PORSCHE 911

ROAD CARS

Dennis Adler
Foreword by Hurley Haywood

MBI Publishing Company

DEDICATION

For Jeanne, who reminds me every day that beauty is timeless. To Dennis Frick for friendship and advice, and to Don Meluzio, Chuck Stoddard, and Kent Rawson for saving the best Porsches.

First published in 1998 by MBI Publishing Company, 729 Prospect Avenue, PO Box 1, Osceola, WI 54020-0001 USA.

MBI Publishing Company books are also available at discounts in bulk quantity for industrial or sales-promotional use. For details write to Special Sales Manager at Motorbooks International Wholesalers & Distributors, 729 Prospect Avenue, Osceola, WI 54020-0001 USA.

Library of Congress Cataloging-in-Publication Data.

Adler, Dennis.
      Porsche 911 road cars/ Dennis Adler.
         p. cm.-- (Sports car color history)
      Includes index.
      ISBN 0-7603-0365-7 (pbk. : alk. paper)
      1. Porsche 911 automobile--History. 2. Porsche 911 automobile--Pictorial works.
      I. Title. II. Series.
    TL215.P75A35 1998
    629.222'2--dc21   97-45035

On the front cover: Air-cooled 911 bookends. In the foreground is a 450-horsepower 1997 911 Turbo S, the fastest, air-cooled, production Porsche ever built. In the background is the 901 preproduction prototype.

On the frontispiece: When the going gets serious, this is the view most other drivers see of Porsche's 911 Turbo Carrera.

On the title page: Early 911s are revered for their simplicity of line and faithfulness to Butzi Porsche's design. The car at the left is Jim Hoffman's 1968 model 911L and the tan car is a 1966 standard 911.

On the back cover: Top: The Touring version of the Carrera RS 2.7 was essentially a 911S interior with the 2.7-liter engine, suspension, and body. This beautiful example is from the Kent Rawson collection. Bottom: Cutaway showing technical details of Porsche's awesome 400 horsepower 1996 Porsche 911 Turbo. *Porsche AG*

Edited by Zack Miller
Designed by Katie L. Sonmor

Printed in Hong Kong through World Print, Ltd.

CONTENTS

FOREWORD

Being part of the Porsche family is very special to the Porsche customer. The traditional blink of the headlights to fellow Porsche drivers gives its owners a sense of pride and exclusiveness.

When you think about what makes a Porsche so special, two things come to mind—design and engineering. If you put 200 cars in a row, your eye will always be able to pick out the 911; it's a classic design, a shape that will never go out of style.

Running parallel with design is engineering. Porsche has always used the race track for ongoing research and development, and the lessons learned have continually improved the production cars. At Porsche, cars are designed and engineered for function and not for any other reason. This has been evident in every 911 since the very first models.

I have raced Porsches for over 25 years, both in Europe and the States, and I have witnessed the evolution of the cars from the early 911 through the present 911 GT 1 race car. With the 911, Porsches went from being consistent class-winning cars to winning overall honors at major international races. For me, it all began when Peter Gregg and I won the 1973 24 Hours of Daytona in a Carrera RS and the 12 Hours of Sebring in a 911 RSR. The RSR later evolved into the awesome 935, which dominated GT racing until the early 1980s. From the 935, we went to the incredible 962, which would dominate racing for the next decade.

I would not have won a record 10 of the endurance classics, which include the 24 Hours of Daytona, the 24 Hours of Le Mans, and the 12 Hours of Sebring, if the Porsches I drove did not have reliability. That same reliability is a part of every 911 road car.

These are complex times in both racing and the world. Finding a clear direction is often more difficult than finding a solution. When I look at what Porsche has done over the 25 years that I have been associated with them, it brings me great pride. When I look at the Boxster and the new 911, I have no doubt that the future looks strong and exciting for Porsche and its old, new, and future customers.

This wonderful new book by author and photographer Dennis Adler is a welcome addition to the volumes written on the history of this amazing automobile.

As for myself, I look for new challenges in the future, and I will always remember that if it were not for Porsche I would not be where I am today.

—*Hurley Haywood*

PREFACE AND ACKNOWLEDGMENTS

"Why would anyone want a Porsche in a town like this?"

It was an interesting question.

This is life in the slow lane, where the romance with the open road is nothing like what you see on television commercials and in the movies, where guys driving exotic sports cars bounce through traffic like a pachinko ball. Yes, occasionally, you get the opportunity to drive at eight-tenths of the car's potential on some open road, or to see how quickly it accelerates from 0 to 60, but most days you live with a sports car in the same world as the Honda Civics and minivans.

The woman asking the question was driving a Volkswagen Cabriolet, her third VW in 10 years. She has two daughters, both VW owners, and her husband has been driving the same Honda Accord since 1991. This intimate exchange, by the way, was being conducted in the number two and number three lanes of the San Diego Freeway at 8:15 A.M. Traffic was at a complete standstill, while the California Highway Patrol and two local wreckers untangled the front of a Lotus Esprit from the underside of a delivery truck. No injuries except to the Lotus owner's insurance policy, which had suffered a fatal impact. You see, in California sheet metal can be easily replaced; an insurance policy can't.

It is the same every morning, seven days a week: tens of thousands of cars heading south from the San Fernando Valley to West L.A. and beyond to Orange County. There are, in the huddled masses, an occasional Ferrari and enough Mercedes-Benzes and BMWs to explain why the Golden State represents one of Germany's most lucrative markets—California alone accounts for more sales than some countries. Across five lanes of concrete, the latest GM and Ford products queue up, along with an overwhelming number of new Chryslers, and a colorful profusion of Japanese and Korean cars—yellows, reds, odd shades of blue and orange, more reds, light browns, pathetic tones of gold, and an abundance of forest green sport utilities. From the news radio chopper overhead, the San Diego Freeway must look as if the Walt Disney studio had blown up.

Author Dennis Adler at rest, momentarily, with Porsche's awesome 911 Turbo.

So why *would* anyone want a Porsche in a town like this? Aside from the customary benefits of 911 ownership, the car is ideally suited for the daily contest, that little game commuters play, in which they gain several car lengths through deft lane changes.

From second gear, the Carrera 4 we're driving comes to life almost immediately, allowing agile maneuvers that lesser cars would never attempt. It is a disturbing fact to many who have not driven a Porsche. What appears to be a sudden and unplanned lane change—and if you can read lips backward through the mirror, a maneuver almost certain to evoke a comment about the driver's resemblance to one of the body's major apertures—is in reality a carefully calculated and quite easily executed move. Other drivers still don't understand. Porsches have an uncanny footing on the road that endows even modestly talented drivers with fine-honed skills ensured by decades of Porsche engineering. In close quarters, more than on the open road, these features are best appreciated.

The remarkable speed of 50 miles per hour has been obtained; the VW Cabriolet becomes a fading white blot in the mirror and then a sea of red lights appears once more. From ahead comes the sound of smoking Michelins. The other side of performance reveals itself—0 to 60 in five-plus seconds is not as important right now as 50 to 0 before the Porsche's slanting nose lodges beneath the elevated rear bumper of a Lincoln Town Car. The Carrera scrubs off speed in an instant with huge, vented, cross-drilled disc brakes. The Volkswagen Cabriolet pulls alongside and then passes. She waves. The Carrera 4 becomes a silver blot in the VW's

mirror. A line from an old Three Stooges comedy comes to mind: "Now we're getting nowhere fast!"

It is at times like this that performance pales in comparison to a good driver's seat and a 10-speaker digital sound system. Porsche has both. Nothing seems more important when you're stirring the shifter from first to second, second to first, and then back to second, than a comfortable seat. The Carrera's is the best Stuttgart has offered since cows started surrendering their hides. Firm where firmness is a must and compliant in those places where legs, hips, and backbones complain.

It would be wonderful to tell tales of 150-mile-per-hour sprints in the Carrera 4, working the six-speed shifter smartly through the pattern and pressing the all-wheel-drive coupe into turns at speeds that would spin mere mortal cars into the guardrail, but it didn't happen. The car's aluminum-alloy flat opposed six never broke a sweat. It didn't overheat in traffic, either. The force-sensitive, power-assist rack-and-pinion steering never came into play. The most difficult maneuver was pulling into a parking space and making certain not to wipe the air dam over the concrete curbing. It was, nevertheless, rewarding. That's the beauty of a Porsche 911, and always has been. You don't need to drive fast to enjoy it. It is a car suited for every situation, be it turning the quarter mile in 13.9 seconds or slugging your way through it in 60. It remains one of the few high-performance sports cars built today that can be considered practical enough for daily driving. In the day-to-day commute, even with the standard gearbox in lieu of Porsche's advanced Tiptronic transmission, shifting is effortless, as is the clutch. On the open road, the 911 can gather speed in breathtaking proportions, corner smartly, predictably, or simply cruise at a leisurely pace. The 911 is perhaps the only sports car ever built that can be described in one word. Perfect.

Since it was first shown at the Frankfurt Auto Show in September 1963, more than 400,000 enthusiastic buyers have agreed, giving the 911 the greatest longevity of any production sports car in history. That's just too hard to explain to someone in a VW when you're stuck in traffic.

It would take a book far larger than this to cover the full history of the Porsche 911 and the men responsible for its 35-year history. What we have done is condense three and a half decades into a pictorial history that chronicles the most significant road cars. Many are rare, others just the basic 911, but each is important to the history of Porsche.

There are few automotive enthusiasts more dedicated to their cars than Porsche collectors, and it is with great appreciation that this book is dedicated to several of them. There are many others who have contributed their time and their cars for the original photography in *Porsche 911 Road Cars*, and without their help and dedication to preserving older 911 models, this book, and the motoring world as well, would be missing some of the most interesting cars to come from the Porsche factory in the 1960s and 1970s. Special thanks to Dennis Frick of German Classic Cars, Bruce Canepa Motor Sports, Joe Vatter and Tech Art, Michael Furman, Ken Kragan, Chad McQueen, Graham Gould, Jim Hoffman, Kurt Hillgruber, and Brad Camp for their time and effort.

Many have followed the road from Zuffenhausen, and there are dozens of books on Porsche history that were used to research background on the models pictured, including the three finest books ever written on Porsche: *Excellence Was Expected*, the bible of Porsche lore, by renowned historian Karl Ludvigsen, without whose work few of us could research the early cars; *Porsche 911 Forever Young*, the highly detailed chronicle of the 911 by Tobias Aichele; and the most recent addition to the telling of the Porsche story, *Porsche Legends* by Randy Leffingwell, who delved further than anyone before into the personal histories of Porsche designers and engineers and the Porsche family.

The creation of a pictorial history also requires the assistance of the manufacturer. All of the archival and factory photography in this book was provided by Porsche AG and the efforts of factory archivist Jens Torner in Stuttgart. All of the new models photographed for the book were provided courtesy of Porsche Cars North America Inc. Our thanks to Bob Carlson and Barbara Manha of PCNA for making so many cars available. And a final note of thanks to Hurley Haywood for sharing his experiences with Porsche and writing the introduction to this book.

It goes without saying that a book requires many people, and while the author may get the credit, it is a collective effort. To everyone who put forth the time to make *Porsche 911 Road Cars* possible, my thanks and appreciation.

—Dennis Adler

CHAPTER ONE

THE ROAD TO ZUFFENHAUSEN

The Source Porsche—Evolution of the 901/911 Prototype

Three decades apart, yet clearly linked by a common design theme that has worked better than any in recent automotive history, the 901 prototype was featured with several different 1994 models for the 911's 30th anniversary. Here it is pictured with a 1994 yellow Carrera 4 Coupe.

The design of the 901 prototype incorporated a number of ideas that did not go into production. One of them was the use of torsion bars to support the trunk lid when it was opened. The thin black torsion bars can be seen across the width of the trunk, attached to the base of the deck lid hinges. It worked all right, just as long as a stiff wind didn't come along and drop the deck lid on your head. The design was later used for the 914 engine lid and rear trunk.

There's an old American saying, "If it ain't broke, don't fix it." It works pretty well in German, too, though it's a bit more difficult to pronounce—"*Man braucht es nicht wieder herstellen, wenn es nicht gebrochen ist.*" Porsche seems to have followed this theory faithfully since 1962, when Ferdinand Alexander "Butzi" Porsche, grandson of the company's founder, designed the 901 prototype.

It has been 35 years since the 901 was introduced, yet the original profile and design of the car has endured, confirming a simple, though difficult to achieve, tenet of design: In simplicity there is beauty. The 911's beauty has lasted long enough to become the most recognized profile in the automotive world.

In his book *Excellence Was Expected*, author Karl Ludvigsen pointed out Butzi Porsche's fears about designing a car that would ostensibly replace the company's only product. The young Porsche joined the family business in 1957, after graduating from the renowned Ulm College of Design. Showing a remarkable talent for styling, he apprenticed under his grandfather's chief stylist, Erwin Franz Komenda, the former deputy director of passenger car design at Daimler-Benz. Komenda joined Porsche in 1931, a year after the company was established by Professor Ferdinand Porsche in the town of Zuffenhausen, just outside Stuttgart, and he had designed every Porsche since the original Gmünd roadster in 1948.

Although the company never manufactured a car until the 356 was introduced in 1948, Porsche established a reputation as one of Germany's leading design studios. Prior to that, Professor Porsche had worked as an engineer and designer for Austro-Daimler, Mercedes & Cie., Daimler-Benz, and Steyr, creating such legendary cars as the 1924 Mercedes, 1927 Mercedes-Benz Type S, 1932 Wanderer, the championship Auto Union race cars, and of course, the Volkswagen.

Under the direction of his son, Ferdinand "Ferry" Porsche, the company rebuilt itself after World War II with the now legendary 356. Thus, it was with some reluctance that Porsche embarked upon the design of a new car to replace the only model the company had ever built. Unlike Ford or General Motors, where an unsuccessful model could be swept under the carpet, a miscalculation by Porsche could cost the company everything.

The original plan for a new model, which would seat four passengers, had been drawn up by Komenda, but Ferry Porsche felt it was too closely tied to the 356, as was Komenda himself. Porsche decided to solicit other designs as well. The first came from renowned stylist Count Albrecht Goertz, an associate of international designer Raymond Loewy. Goertz designed the stunning 507 for BMW in 1955, and his work was highly regarded in Germany. His approach to a 356 replacement, however, was too American in design. In Ferry Porsche's words, "A beautiful Goertz, but not a Porsche."

By 1959 Butzi was working on his own design, which was completed as a plasticine model in October. A full-scale version was finished by December 28, his entire crew having worked through Christmas to have a final design study ready by year's end. Although there were several other proposals from Komenda, the design for the 901 prototype was ultimately based on Butzi Porsche's proposal.

Already an accomplished designer by the age of 28, when he became head of the Styling Department at Porsche, Butzi was willing to bend, if not rewrite the rules of established Porsche design, and by 1961 he was ready to finalize the body lines and engineering for Porsche's successor to the aging 356.

The problem Butzi had to address from the beginning of the project was one of propriety. "Must you build a new Porsche just like the old one, as Komenda had suggested?" In

Firsts and lasts. Beginnings and endings. It's the stuff that automotive history is made of. And this is both—the only known surviving 901 preproduction prototype and the first road-going example of what was to become the legendary 911. The car is pictured with a 1997 Turbo S, 34 years newer, but unmistakably evolved from the 901.

The 901 engine cover is supported by two long springs with a multihole bracket for tension adjustment. The squared-off air cleaner is similar to those on early production cars, and the rear cross-member is flat instead of the indented production panel. The 901's original engine (No. 900014) and transmission were replaced at some time in the past. In November 1964 the car was converted to production parts and used for additional testing by the factory.

many respects, the answer was yes, but Butzi wrote, "It should be a new Porsche . . . as good as or better than the old, and in the same pattern, but not necessarily the same form." What exactly did that mean? One has only to compare an early 911 with a late model 356 coupe to find the answer. The 911 was a virtual extension of the 356 design—longer, sleeker, more powerful, but quintessentially Porsche. The trademark lines were still evident. Butzi accomplished what no one, even the legendary Komenda, had been able to do: recreate the Porsche in its own image.

Although developmental changes to the engine, suspension, transmission, and interior continued until the first prototype 901 was shown in August 1963, and even afterwards, the body design proposed by Butzi Porsche in December 1961, known as the Type 644 T8, was the foundation upon which all further development of the 901 was carried out. This led to one of the company's most difficult and historically pivotal business decisions.

Karosserie Reutter in Stuttgart, which had produced nearly all of the coachwork for the Porsche 356, announced that it was

unwilling to spend the money necessary to retool for a completely new body design, and in fact decided to sell the coach-building branch of the company in Zuffenhausen. They kept the original Stuttgart facility, forming the Recaro GmbH and Company, to continue making seats and seat adjusters. Since the Reutter coachworks and Porsche factory were both in Zuffenhausen, and Porsche had been the company's primary client since 1951, Porsche seemed the likely candidate to buy Reutter. It was a decision the Porsche family considered at some length before deciding to purchase Karosseriewerk Reutter in July 1963. This was to become the first real financial burden on the Porsche family since the early postwar years, when Ferry and his sister Louise Piëch had established a temporary factory in the rustic Austrian village of Gmünd. It was there that the very first Porsche sports cars were built in 1948.

After Porsche took over the Reutter operation, it began the process of retooling for the all-new 901 body. As demand for the cars increased following the 1964 model introduction, however,

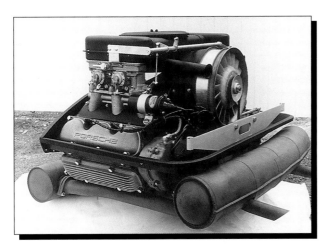

Factory photo of the Type 901 engine with official designation, six-cylinder, 2.0-liter, 130 horsepower. The picture was taken of an early preproduction motor in 1963. The 901/1 1,991-cc flat six was designed by Ferdinand Piëch, Ferry Porsche's nephew, and Hans Tomala. In 1965, Piëch took charge of the research and development departments at Porsche. The eight-main bearing engine had an oversquare design with an 80-millimeter x 66-millimeter (3.15-inch x 2.60-inch) bore and stroke. Output was rated at 130 horsepower at 6,100 rpm with 140 foot-pounds of torque at 4,200 rpm.

Porsche also relied on Wilhelm Karmann GmbH in Osnabrück to build additional 911 bodies, as demand outstripped the Reutter factory's capabilities.

Change within the European automotive community was always a long process, and for Porsche this was particularly true. There was still considerable doubt right up to the end as to whether the 356 should be replaced (the 356C remained in production for more than a year after the 911 was introduced). To ensure that Porsche could gauge public and media reaction to the 901, it was shown at the Frankfurt Auto Show in September 1963, a full year before it was to go on sale. Even though the response was more than favorable, Porsche still felt the need to justify its actions in print. A press release announcing the introduction of a new model to replace the venerable 356 explained the "theory" behind the design and development of the 901.

"For years Ferry Porsche and his team of engineers have racked their brains as to how to keep the Porsche motto 'Driving in its purest form' both up to date and in tune with the constantly changing conditions of modern traffic."

The press release explained that Porsche's goal in creating a successor for the 356 was to design ". . . a car with hardly larger outside measurements than the present one and yet one with more interior room. It should have an engine that can cope without strain with today's traffic jam . . . yet possess the performance of the Carrera—lightning acceleration to a maximum speed of over 200 kilometers per hour(120 miles per hour). Apart from that, it should have an easily accessible luggage compartment. To that should be added the roadholding of a sports car plus the comfort of the Gran Turismo for the long journey. Equally necessary was a Porsche synchronized, properly spaced, five-speed gearbox, as well as the highest quality bodywork, and all this within a reasonable price." A description that still suits the 911 after 35 years, with the possible exception of "reasonable price."

The 901 embodied more changes than the company had ever made, from the body and interior, right down to the final suspension layout and new overhead cam, six-cylinder boxer engine—the foundation of every 911 motor to the present. The new powerplant retained Porsche's established air/oil-cooling system and horizontally opposed layout, but now had overhead camshafts driven by double-row roller chains. The two-cam 901's 130-horsepower output matched that of the four-cam 356 Carrera 2, without the requisite mechanical complexity.

Porsche continued to use the 356's torsion bar suspension, but modified its execution in the 901. Up front, MacPherson struts replaced double trailing arms, with the front torsion bars sent lengthwise instead of transversely, inside the A-arm, allowing more trunk space. The 901 engineering team moved the steering mechanism—now a rack-and-pinion design—toward the center of the car, using an offset double-jointed shaft. This also proved to be a safer design in the event of a severe frontal collision, eliminating the possibility of the steering column being pushed through into the driver's seat . . . and presumably through the driver.

The new 901 measured up as both a larger and a smaller car compared to its predecessor. The wheelbase was some 104 millimeters longer, to provide additional footroom and larger rear seats—although rear accommodations were never seriously considered appropriate for anything but a short drive. The 901's greater wheelbase did have one notable advantage, however: longer doors that allowed easier entry and exit. The upper body was wider to increase hip and shoulder room, while the passing of the 356's "bathtub" physique allowed the 901's exterior to decrease in width by almost 3 inches. From end to end, the 901 was some 5 inches longer than the 356.

By any account, the 901 was a stunning success, continuing the traditions established by Porsche with the 356 series, but at the same time, creating a new following: a cadre of owner/enthusiasts who made this one of the most coveted sports cars of all time.

Whenever Porsche enthusiasts gather, there are always "stories" to be told, and one of the more interesting pieces of 911 lore is the reason for Porsche's famous 11th-hour name change. The production version was originally badged just as the prototype, 901, and the lower-priced four-cylinder model was to be named the 902. How they became the 911 and 912 is a story few people outside of Porsche actually know. The facts,

On the 901 the rear valance/bumper was one piece incorporating the bumper and license plate panel. Production 911s had a three-piece design comprising two bumpers (left and right) and a license plate panel in between.

The interior of 13 327 is upholstered in black with houndstooth seat inserts. Americans never really cared for the houndstooth fabric, which was popular with Europeans. This was the customary upholstery for the 901/911 unless otherwise specified. The sliding roof in 13 327 was an experimental design that was never put into production. The manually operated panel was designed to move forward rather than backward and then tilt up to serve as a wind deflector. With the hand crank actually mounted on the moving panel, the design served little purpose and was definitely an unusual concept.

though not nearly as romantic as some of the stories that have been told over the years, are nonetheless intriguing.

First, the 901 designation had nothing to do with the car's design, as is often rumored. In the early 1960s, Porsche was more closely integrating its sales and service with Volkswagen (the controlling families of both concerns were intertwined through marriage), and Porsche simply needed parts numbers that would be compatible with VW's. The next available series

From behind the wheel (adapted from the 356 series for this prototype), this is almost an entirely different car from the production model. In place of the standard 911's familiar five-dial instrument grouping are two large gauges with switches on either side. The gauges were of unknown source and had hand-painted graphics on the tachometer. They were larger than 356 gauges by some 50 millimeters, making them 150 millimeters (6 inches) in diameter. Whether this design was actually considered is not known. Several configurations were used on the 901 test cars, including one that closely resembled the final design, with five round instruments.

Porsche number 13 327—the oldest 911 in existence—sits on a wheelbase of 86.8 inches (2,204 millimeters). In the late 1960s, Porsche increased the wheelbase to 89.3 inches (2,268 millimeters). Front and rear track are 52.4 inches (1,332 millimeters) and 51.7 inches (1,312 millimeters), respectively. Overall length is 162.8 inches (4,135 millimeters). At 168.3 inches (4,275 millimeters), today's cars are nearly 6 inches longer. The 911 was about 5 inches longer than the 356. This Type 901 prototype was restored by Dennis Frick's firm, German Classic Cars of New Cumberland, Pennsylvania, for Porsche collector Don Meluzio.

Butzi Porsche poses with one of the 901 prototypes in 1963. His original design for the car, completed in October 1959, was the basis for the now legendary 911 series. *Porsche AG*

at Volkswagen began with 900, thus the new model would be 901. It would have remained so but for an unexpected encounter with Peugeot in September 1964.

The first 901 prototype was shown at the Frankfurt International Automobile Show in September 1963. A year later another of the prototypes was exhibited at the Paris Auto Salon, and much to the surprise of those at Porsche, the company was contacted by Peugeot's legal department, which informed Porsche that the French auto maker had been using three numeral designations for all of its passenger cars—two numbers with a zero between them—since 1929! Therefore, 901 would be a Peugeot model designation, and under French trademark regulations Peugeot held the exclusive rights to the use of such model names in France! Porsche had to change the name of the car if it was to be sold in France. Since the French export market was vital to Porsche's European sales, and the cars were already in production, a swift resolution was necessary. The name was simply changed from 901 to 911 (and the four-cylinder 902, introduced in 1965, to 912), although

901 and 902 were still used internally for factory designations of engines and part numbers. The official name change came on November 10, 1964, with chassis number 300 049. The first production 911s were not delivered until afterward, even though 49 cars had already been built with the official designation 901.

Now you might ask, "What about the Porsche 904?" Since it was a competition car and had already been on the market unbeknownst to Peugeot for nearly a year (one wonders how Peugeot couldn't have known!), the company was willing to grant an exception. Porsche capitalized on this concession by using the middle zero for competition models through the 909. Nothing was ever heard from Peugeot again.

THE 901 PROTOTYPES

Porsche reserved 10 "replacement chassis" numbers, beginning with the prefix 13, for preproduction cars. To the consternation of most Porsche authorities, however, the company contradicts itself by listing a total of thirteen 901 prototypes in its anniversary compilation of 911 models! The confusion may have been a result of early production cars that were also used for testing. Officially, there are only 10 developmental cars with the number 13 prefix. The first was chassis 13 321 nicknamed *Sturmvogel* (Storm Petrel) followed by 13 322, known as *Fledermaus* (Bat); 13 323, nicknamed *Blaumeise* (Blue Titmouse); 13 324, called *Zitronenfalter* (Brimstone Butterfly); and 13 325, which went nameless.

Of the remaining six test cars (serial numbers 13 326, 13 327, 13 328, 13 330, 13 352, 300 001, and 300 002, the last two being production car serial numbers), chassis number 13 327 (featured in the color photos in this chapter) built in 1963 and nicknamed *Barbarossa*, is the only restored 901 known to exist.

Although Porsche has always prided itself on cars that were "made by hand," nowhere is it more evident than on this 901 prototype. With the 901, there was nothing, save for minor items, that could be carried over from the 356. The chassis, engine, driveline, interior, and suspension all had to be made and assembled by hand for the prototypes.

The first show car, 13 325, was painted yellow and featured Porsche's traditional houndstooth fabric upholstery and vinyl trim. It premiered in Frankfurt along with the latest 356C Coupe and Cabriolet, also making their 1963 debut. (The 911's formal introduction was a year away, and the 356 was still in production.)

After the Frankfurt show, three additional 901 show cars were completed. According to factory records, prototype chassis 13 326, known as Quick Blue, was used by Ferdinand Piëch after it toured the 1963–1964 auto shows in London, Sweden, Berlin, and Geneva. Piëch kept his car until the end of 1965, after which it was sold to a Porsche employee, Hans Mezger, and later to a private party in Stuttgart. There is no record of 13 326 after 1967. It is also believed that at least one of the four show cars was disassembled, run through the 911 production line, and sold as a new car.

Photographs of the Porsche display at the 1964 Geneva Auto Show include not only a 904 but in the background what might well be chassis 13 327, rather than chassis 13 326. Through early 1965, it was used as a test vehicle, evident on the restored car's chassis and body, which have countless patched openings where different components, hoses, and ducts were apparently routed and then rerouted by the engineering staff as they experimented with various ideas.

In April 1965, ownership of 13 327 was transferred to *Christophorus* magazine editor Richard von Frankenberg, an accomplished race driver and automotive journalist who had been with Porsche since 1950. He is perhaps best remembered, both pictorially and in Lawrence Braun's sculpture, *Miracle of the Avus*, for having survived a spectacular crash at the Avus Ring in 1956. Having careened over the lip of the track's north curve, von Frankenberg was thrown clear of his car moments before it crashed to the ground on the other side of the wall. He landed in the bushes and suffered only minor injuries. Fate was on his side that day. Not so 17 years later, when he was killed in a road accident.

The von Frankenberg 901 ended up in Italy and then surfaced a decade later in New York City, where it was discovered wasting away in a service garage. At the time, the car was thought to be a cobbled up mixture of 911 and 356 parts, its history unknown until research by Paul Resnick revealed that the odd-looking 911 he had purchased was actually a 901 prototype. In 1984, he advertised the car in *Porsche Panorama* and sold it to present owner Don Meluzio, a Porsche racer and Chrysler dealer in York, Pennsylvania. The car was turned over to Porsche specialist Dennis Frick and his staff at German Classic Cars in New Cumberland, Pennsylvania, for a ground-up restoration, a project that took several long years to complete.

"In design there is styling, art, and other terms intermingled," commented Butzi Porsche in Randy Leffingwell's book, *Porsche Legends*. "Design means to me that every designing engineer has the opportunity to become at some stage an artist . . . that every craftsman who can do more than what he is trained to do is an artist." As a designer, Butzi was an artist; in designing the 901 there was a progression of scale models that allowed Porsche and his staff to, as he said, "Feel it, touch it, work on it." *Porsche AG*

Butzi had already designed the Type 718 coupe of 1961 and the Porsche 904 in 1963, both of which lent a little of their styling to the 901. The 904, more so than the 911, became Butzi Porsche's signature car, just as the 300SL became Rudolph Uhlenhaut's at Mercedes-Benz and the 507 that of Albrecht Goertz at BMW.

A full-scale version of Butzi Porsche's proposal for a model to replace the venerable 356 was finished by December 28, 1959, his entire crew having worked through Christmas to have a final design study ready by year's end. Although there were several other proposals, Butzi Porsche's prototype design, known as the T7, was ultimately the foundation upon which all future design work was based.

With the Frankfurt debut of the 901 just two months away, road testing of disguised cars was being conducted in July 1963. This is the first 901 prototype, photographed by Porsche while making a run between Weilimdorf and Münchingen on July 10. *Porsche AG*

One of the early 901 prototypes photographed in 1963. This car had the transverse grille favored by the styling department as a solution to the rear air inlet design. In all, there were six proposals created by Butzi Porsche. *Porsche AG*

Dr. Ferdinand "Ferry" Porsche (right) and his son, Ferdinand Alexander "Butzi" Porsche III, pose with an early 911 and a 1993 model for the company's 30th anniversary celebration of the 911. *Porsche AG*

As he explains it, Frick had to put himself in the position of an engineer assembling a hand-built prototype. "A prototype is different from a production car," he says. "The 901 was obviously the object of extensive experimentation, and over time several different, mutually exclusive heating and ventilation systems had been installed. When they were removed, the openings were simply patched and painted over."

Restoring the 901 to its original condition meant keeping these idiosyncracies intact, virtually restoring the damage that had been done to the car during development and testing!

"Getting into this car," recalls Frick, "was like trying to assemble a puzzle when you don't know what the picture looks like!" The doorsills and seat rails were all handmade, with abandoned seat mounting holes and file marks in evidence. The body exhibited dimensional differences from side to side, "as if the guy working on the right never spoke to the guy working on the left," says Frick, with an almost knowing look in his eyes.

Working on the car, he discovered that many off-the-shelf, or possibly off-the-floor, 356 parts were used for the prototype's construction. For example, a passenger-assist handle from the 356C model is attached to the right A pillar. The steering wheel and horn ring were taken directly from a 356, as were the window cranks. A fresh air handle was made from a T6 hand throttle. The braking system was taken over nearly unchanged from the last of the 356 line, the 356C.

One area of the 911 that exhibited a number of modifications from the 901 prototype was the exhaust system and rear valance design. On the prototype, the muffler and exhaust pipes rubbed the ground when the cars were driven up a steep grade. To correct this, Porsche notched the lower panel to provide more clearance for the exhaust pipes. This temporary fix worked for the show cars, but in production, the exhaust system was altered to a single outlet and the valance changed from a one-piece design incorporating the license plate panel to three individual pieces comprising of two bumperettes and a license plate insert.

An excellent example of a factory key fob with the embossed Porsche crest. The cars were originally supplied with the leather key fobs. Few have survived.

The more things change, the more they remain the same. Sure it's a clichè, but just because something is clichè doesn't mean it isn't true. Take the simple Porsche fuel filler: 35 years later, it is still the same basic design and in the exact same place!

Prototypes often have features that are merely for appearances; in other words, they don't work. For example, the 901 had fixed quarter windows. On the first 911 production cars they swung open for ventilation; however, years later, when heating and ventilation systems improved, Porsche returned to the 901's original fixed quarter window design.

Behind the wheel, this is almost an entirely different car. In place of the 911's instrument grouping are two large gauges with switches positioned on either side. The two big dials demanded a higher dash and a different panel configuration; however, this was not the only design. The Frankfurt show car had an instrument array similar to the final production version of the 911, so the gauges in 13 327 may have been simply another idea that Porsche was considering. The two-gauge design was also used on Butzi Porsche's Type 695 T7 concept car.

The 901's doors, although similar to production versions, have several uncommon features. For example, the vent windows have an internal pivot, rather than the later frame-mounted hinges. Next to each vent window is a small hole in the doorsill cap, which was intended to be a defroster vent. The inside door handles are heavy painted steel, hinged below the

Hoodlines have remained almost the same on the 911 for more than 30 years. The silver car is a 1997 model.

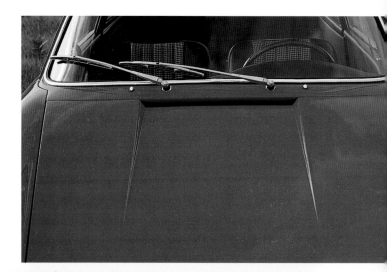

armrest and at best difficult to find. The latches are the same as those used on a period VW Karmann-Ghia.

Of course, all of these differences are minor. The 901's basic shape hardly changed from Butzi Porsche's original design, and only slight alterations to the exterior were tried—a round fuel filler flap, for example, on 13 327, instead of an oval one. There is no trim along the rockers, the door handles are skinnier than normal (prototype pieces made from solid brass), there are no bumper overriders up front, and

even the P O R S C H E script on the rear deck lid is different, taken directly from a late-model 356. The list goes on, from torsion bars used to support the trunk lid, to a hand-built fuel tank welded together from 20 individual steel panels. Yet when you park it alongside a production 911, there are far more similarities than differences. The 911 has gone through many changes since the 901 prototype—ever-increasing engine size and power output, ground-breaking developments in fuel injection and engine management technology, turbocharging and intercooling, the development of high-performance automatic transmissions, all-wheel drive, brakes that rank among the finest in the world, and handling improvements that would embarrass the fastest race

The dashboard and instrument design of the 901 prototype gave way to a final layout with five gauges, shown in the factory mockup, photographed in 1964. The 1997 model, with special "brick"-colored interior, still maintains the original 1964 model's design, right down to the traditional left-hand, dash-mounted key switch.

Even the passing of 35 years and numerous changes in the styling of the 911 fenderline and headlight treatment haven't altered the basic appearance of the car as designed by Butzi Porsche.

Taillights have changed over the years, but the styling is still reminiscent of the original 901 design.

cars of 1963. Yet at a glance, few of them are obvious. What *is* conspicuous is the heritage and sense of history that every model carries with it, that unmistakable Porsche 911 profile.

The 1998 Carrera, which is the final evolution of the original air-cooled, rear-engined Porsche design, has the same uncommon simplicity, call it familiarity, as every 911 produced over the past 35 years, right down to an ignition switch still located to the left of the steering wheel. Slipping into the driver's seat of this car is fundamentally no different from that of any 911 built since 1963.

How does a company that seems to go from strength to strength continue to reinvent itself without really changing? It is a skill that Porsche alone seems to have perfected. Or perhaps Porsche has simply adopted as doctrine Alphonse Karr's often-quoted saying: "The more things change, the more they remain the same."

Horsepower has certainly increased, from the 901's 130 horsepower to the Carrera 4's 270-horsepower output, but the engine configuration is still the same flat, opposed design introduced on the 901.

CHAPTER TWO

THE EARLY 911 MODELS

Porsche Throughout the 1960s and Early 1970s

The earliest 911 models were perhaps the purest in their faithfulness to Butzi Porsche's design. Pictured is a 1966 model 911 (tan) and a 1968 model 911L. The 1966 example was equipped with optional leather upholstery, fog lights, and AM/FM SW Frankfurt radio. The 911L came equipped with an electric sunroof.

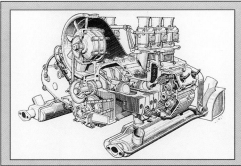

This factory drawing shows the detail of the Type 901 engine as seen from the rear of the car. At left are the twin pumps for the Solex carburetors, at the top is the axial cooling fan, and at the bottom, built around the exhaust manifolds, are the exchangers to provide interior heating. The horizontally opposed engine layout used crossflow hemispherical combustion chambers.

The 911 was the ideal sports car. From the beginning, it was quick, easy to drive, reasonably comfortable, and not terribly complicated; the kind of sports car most people only dream of owning. Not as exotic as a Ferrari, nor even a Jaguar, but not afflicted with any of their shortcomings either. It was a work of art, aesthetically and mechanically, but so subtly packaged that only those who drove the 911 came to appreciate it to the fullest. The new Porsche was not so much a driver's car as it was an owner's car.

Despite being more luxurious than the 356, and ostensibly a four-passenger model (although the rear seatbacks were most always folded down to provide greater storage space), the 911 was far better suited to the dual roles of sports car and boulevardier than its decade-old predecessor.

Porsche had bet everything on the 911, and now with the 356 gone, the company's future was in the hands of automotive writers and customers who would weigh the new car against the old, a model that had in its short history become almost legendary as both road car and race car. To Porsche's relief, the world motor press, often the greatest critics of change, celebrated the 911 with accolades. Wrote *Car and Driver*, "Race breeding and engineering ooze from the 911's every pore. The whole package, especially the powertrain, is designed to be more reliable and less difficult to service." Concluded the magazine in glowing praise, ". . . it's worth the price of all the old Porsches put together. More importantly, the 911's appeal should be considerably wider than the earlier models." The same was heard from every major American and European automotive journal, few of which had any idea just how many years had gone into the design and development of the new Porsche.

The car's greatest appeal, at least in the early years, was its styling more than its performance, decisively proven by sales of the companion 912. When the lower-priced, four-cylinder model made its debut late in 1964, effectively replacing the 356C in Europe (although the bathtub remained available until September 1965 for sale in the United States), the 912 became Porsche's best-selling car. What greater testimony could there have been to Butzi Porsche's design! During 1966, the first full year in which the 911 and 912 were built together, Porsche sold more than 9,000 912s compared to around 4,000 911s. By year's end sales of more than 1,000 cars a month had made Porsche's 911 and 912 the most popular sports cars on the market, particularly in the United States.

The 911 quickly found its way into the hands of motorsports enthusiasts, (just as the 356 had in the early 1950s) and Porsche 911s immediately acquitted themselves in competition. In 1966, drivers steering 911s around the world's toughest road courses earned sports car championships in West Germany, Austria, Spain, and America. Among those titles was the SCCA Class D Production trophy, won by Jerry Titus in a car sponsored by Los Angeles Porsche dealer Vasek Polak. Porsche 911s also collected their share of trophies in European hill-climb events, and in 1966, a 911 finished 14th in the 24 Heures du Mans. The car was driven to and from Le Mans on the road. (During this same period the Porsche factory works cars, the 904 and 906, were also claiming victories in Grand Prix races and hill climbs, putting Porsche at the forefront of international motorsports).

The next step in Butzi Porsche's plan for the 911 was a convertible model. A cabriolet version was on the drawing board from the beginning, but here again there was a hurdle. A true cabriolet required a redesigned rear shape and a lower windshield, and the economies of manufacturing on a small scale would not allow such a major sheet metal change. There had to be another way of creating an open 911. Butzi Porsche's solution became one of the company's greatest trademarks.

The original production version of the 901/1 engine delivered 130 brake horsepower at 6,100 rpm. The boxer engine used a forged-steel crankshaft with eight main bearings. A countershaft mounted beneath carried drive to twin chain sprockets at the crank's rear end, each sprocket driving a camshaft. Ahead of the countershaft were two oil pumps: a large scavenger for circulating oil between the dry sump and a separate, remote reservoir and a small pump for maintaining oil pressure. An oil cooler was also used since the engine relied upon lubricants to aid overall cooling.

At the 1965 Frankfurt show Porsche unveiled a unique car with a lift-off roof panel above the front seats and a narrow roof structure covering the rear, which, though eliminating the back quarter windows, allowed the car to have the same profile as the coupe. The new model was called the Targa, and like Carrera, it too was a name rich in racing history—taken from the famous Targa Florio road race in Sicily.

The Targa design, emphasized by its wide, brushed stainless steel integral roll bar, solved a number of styling and structural problems all at once and gave Porsche yet another safety feature. The structural integrity of the Targa bar made the 911 the safest production convertible on the road for rollover protection, a factor Porsche considered because it feared U.S. regulations would someday eliminate open vehicles without rollover protection. While this was still some time before the Congressional Safety/Emissions hearings began in Washington, rumors of legislation that would run convertibles off the road were rife throughout the auto industry. Porsche was perhaps reacting

prematurely, but responsibly, by addressing the issue of safety long before it became a government mandate, which, of course, never happened. Still, this mostly unsubstantiated belief brought an end to the American convertible market by the mid-1970s and for nearly a decade after.

The Targa was made available in both 911 and 912 models, and to Porsche's surprise was far more popular than expected. The cars sold as quickly as they arrived in dealer showrooms. In no time there were back orders and waiting periods for delivery. All Porsche had to do now was follow its own history and continue to develop the 911 along the same lines as the 356. It was time for the engineers to have their say.

There have always been two factions within Porsche, the designers and the engineers, and often they did not agree. In the days of Erwin Komenda, the two were more closely tied, but with the 911 there were always two sides. Now that the 911 had proven itself, a demand quickly arose for a more powerful engine, and just as Porsche had bowed to the pleas of sports car enthusiasts in the 1950s by introducing the four-cam Carrera motor for the 1955 356A model line, Zuffenhausen again offered its clientele a sportier model. This time it was less difficult, however. The 911 engine, which was designed by Ferry Porsche's nephew, Ferdinand Piëch, and engineer Hans Tomala, was very conservative in its displacement and output. Increasing the swept volume of the flat six and boosting horsepower was the next logical step.

The first new model came toward the end of 1966; it was called the 911S—S denoting Super, just as it had in the 356 line. Explains Joe Vatter, a former Porsche factory mechanic, "The 911S became the flagship model. This was a high-performance version of the 901/1 engine with a different cam profile, larger valves, better porting, larger jets on the Weber carburetors, and a higher compression ratio (9.8:1 versus 9.0:1)." The net result was an increase in output of 30 brake horsepower, enough to make the 911S a very competitive rally car.

At a glance it was hard to distinguish a 912 from a 911. The 912 was powered by the 356C (1600SC) four-cylinder engine, making the car less potent on the road but far, far more affordable than the 911. In the first full year of production, Porsche delivered 9,090 Type 912 models, roughly half of which were sold in the United States. Introduced in late 1964 as a 1965 model, the 912 did not go on sale in the United States until June 1965, as a 1966 model. *Porsche AG*

A blast from the past, fashions and hair courtesy of 1967. This is a factory photo of the 1967 model 911S 2.0 coupe. Note the polished Fuchs wheels and rear windshield wiper. Like its 356 predecessor, the 911 models featured fully independent suspensions. Up front, Porsche used MacPherson struts on single transverse A-arms connecting to longitudinal torsion bars. At the rear, semi-trailing arms and transverse torsion bars were used in place of the 356's VW-based swing-axle design. *Porsche AG*

The Targa was designer Butzi Porsche's solution to a convertible version of the 911 without the significant cost of retooling for a different body. Although he would have preferred to do just that, as it turned out, the Targa became a sensation and a design that remained in production for nearly 30 years. The scale model shown with Butzi in 1968 shows the original design with the zip-out rear window. The plastic windows did not prove to be an asset, and in 1969 the Targas were equipped with a fixed-glass rear window, which also allowed for an electric defroster. *Porsche AG*

Factory photo of the 911S engine in 1969. This is the 2.0-liter engine (901/10) introduced in 1969, which increased output from 160 brake horsepower to 170 brake horsepower through the use of Bosch mechanical port injection and an increase in compression ratio from 9.8:1 to 9.9:1. *Porsche AG*

Realizing that the 911S was likely to be embraced by competition-minded customers, Porsche also improved the suspension by adding a rear antiroll bar, Koni shock absorbers, ventilated disc brakes all around, and a revised five-speed transmission geared to take full advantage of the added horsepower and torque. The cars were also distinct in their use of boldly forged Fuchs aluminum wheels, which quickly became a trademark of the 911S. As a sports car in the hands of skilled drivers, the 911S was remarkable; as a street car, however, it was not the best choice, with a propensity to swap ends if driven improperly into a corner. Wrote *Road & Track*, ". . . it's easier to hang out the tail if you're in the right gear, simply because of the increased power. But the simple application of steering to the 911S at highway speeds gets the same results as in the 911, which means stick-stick-stick-oversteer! And you'd better know what you're doing in that last phase."

The most powerful Porsche of the 1960s, the 911S, was introduced in 1966. The example pictured is a 1973 model with the 2.4-liter engine. This is a totally original 26,000-mile car. The driving lights, sunroof, and rear wiper are the only options on the car. No longer the flagship of the Porsche line, the 911S was second to the all-new RS 2.7 in 1973. This was to be the last year for the original 911 body style. The beautiful long nose of the 911 had to be shortened in 1974 to accommodate the 5-mile-per-hour impact bumpers mandated by new U.S. safety standards. The bumpers changed both the front and rear appearance of the 911, marking the first significant change in the body design since 1963. Although the bumpers were only required for U.S. cars, Porsche chose to redesign the 911 for the world market.

The 911S interior for 1973 features the traditional European houndstooth seat inserts and black interior. Although this was the most luxurious and powerful model in the Porsche line, 911 interiors at this point in time were still not far beyond the basic design of the original 1964 production models.

Car and Driver, long known for thrashing the best performance out of a car, managed to clock 0 to 60 in the 911S in a record 6.5 seconds, the quarter mile in 15.2, and reach a top speed of 140 miles per hour. *Road & Track* turned in a rather lengthy 8.1-second clip to 60 miles per hour and clocked the quarter mile in 15.7 seconds, attaining 141 miles per hour. The well-known European motoring journal *Autocar* reported 8.0 seconds to 60, 15.8 in the quarter, and a top speed of 137 miles per hour. *Road & Track* also applauded the car's "sparkling acceleration" and long-winded torque curve that "at about 3,000 takes a deep breath and literally surges up to the next step, where the extra punch feels like an additional pair of cylinders being switched in."

The 911S was fast; however, it was not an ideal car for the city, tending to foul plugs more readily than even the normal 911, which itself had a consistent problem with carbon build-up if driven routinely in slow traffic. Nonetheless, all three publications praised the 911S for its many virtues, making only small note of the car's shortcomings. Con-

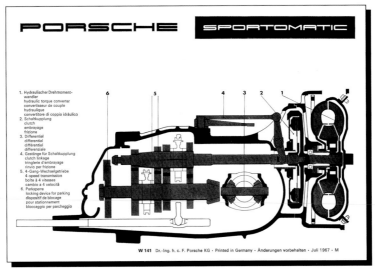

AS this line drawing illustrates, the Sportomatic gearbox, introduced in 1967, was one of the 911's most unusual options. Devised by Fitchtel & Sachs, it was a modern-day revival of the semi-automatic transmissions Detroit automakers had dreamed up a decade before. The F&S used a vacuum servo to disengage the clutch automatically (hence no clutch pedal) as soon as the driver touched the shifter. Its sensitivity to movement required as deft a hand at gear change as a traditional clutch, since the driver had to lift off the gas at precisely the right moment to avoid over-revving the engine. The worst part was the occasional, inadvertent bumping of the shifter, which knocked the car out of gear and over-revved the engine. *Porsche AG*

system was a clutchless shifter, a revival of sorts of the old semi-automatic transmissions Detroit automakers dreamed up in the 1950s. Only they didn't work. Sportomatic did, unless one had a penchant for fingering the shifter while driving. You couldn't because touching the shifter activated the vacuum servo unit that disengaged the clutch. To change up or down through the four-speed synchro, one simply touched the shifter and moved it into the next gear. The only caution was to make certain your foot was off the gas before you activated the servo, otherwise the engine would immediately over-rev. It was half the

cluded *Road & Track*, ". . . a superb GT car . . . everything a Porsche should be—and more." *Car and Driver* described the 911S as Porsche's "all-time high." In 1966 there was little in the way of a road-going sports car that could match the 911S, at least nothing this side of a Ferrari or an E-Type Jaguar. The 911S remained Porsche's high-performance leader until the beginning of the Rennsport era in the 1970s.

Not all Porsche owners were looking for an adrenaline rush every time they got behind the wheel. Recalling a line from its original mission statement in 1963, ". . . the roadholding of a sports car plus the comfort of the Gran Turismo for the long journey," Porsche introduced the 911L. The *L* stood for *Luxus* (luxury), and for the additional $600 above the price of a base 911 owners received every feature of the 911S, except for the high-performance engine. At the other end of the scale, Porsche also had the 911T, a lower-priced Touring model with a detuned 110-horsepower engine and the basic interior and exterior features of the 911. Porsche had re-established its old three-tier marketing system with a car in each price and performance classification, this in addition to the 912 coupe and 912 Targa.

One of the few oddities in the 911's history was the addition of a new transmission in 1967 known as the Sportomatic. Devised by Fitchtel & Sachs (which manufactured clutches for Porsche) the

process of shifting with a clutch, but required more concentration to coordinate the shift and gas pedal movement timing.

While the Sportomatic worked, and received favorable reviews from most of the automotive magazines (*Car and Driver* hated it), the idea never really caught on, especially in the United States. The car was actually much more popular in Europe. *Sports Car Graphic* probably summed up the opinion of most Americans on the Sportomatic by writing, "Give me stick shift or give me death." The Sportomatic worked better than most gave it credit for, however. In August 1967 a 911R Sportomatic driven by Vic Elford, Hans Herrmann, and Jochen Neerpasch, won the grueling 84-hour Marathon de la Route—350 trips around the 17.58-mile Nürburgring course, proving the durability of the design. At around the same time, a semi automatic transmission of similar design was being used in Can-Am racing by Jim Hall and Chaparral. Still, there were not many takers and the Sportomatic became something of an unmentionable in Porsche circles. It remained a special order option through May 1979. A restored 911 Sportomatic is a rare find these days.

As the 1960s came to a close, Porsche had its trio of models ideally sorted out. For 1969 there was the 911T developing 110 brake horsepower and offering the basic interior and trim; the 911E, replacing the 911L as the luxury version, now with an

Beginning with the 1972 model year, the 911 engine was increased in swept volume to 2,341 cc through a change in stroke to 70.4 millimeters (bore remained at 84 millimeters). The rear deck lid bore the numbers 2.4—a bit of a stretch. Output for the 911S was rated at 190 brake horsepower at 6,500 rpm. The 911S had a compression ratio of 8.5:1. Fuel delivery was by Bosch mechanical port injection.

output of 140 brake horsepower; and the flagship 911S delivering 170 brake horsepower. Beginning with the 1969 models, the 911E and 911S were equipped with Bosch fuel injection, while the 911T drew its fuel from twin Weber 40 IDTs. Porsche had also eliminated the 911's plug-fouling problems with the Bosch HKZ high-voltage capacitor ignition system. The Bosch HKZ gave both a higher spark voltage at the plug, for starting and high-speed running, and a faster, steeper voltage rise at the plug electrodes, ensuring that less energy would dissipate over the surface of a dirty plug.

The general configuration of the 911 changed little. The new models had slightly flared wheel openings to cover wider brakes that had expanded the track by 0.4 inch, the 911S had larger 6-inch-wide wheels, and all 911 "B" series cars rode on a slightly longer wheelbase, increased by 57 millimeters (2.28 inches) to accommodate longer rear semi trailing arms and make future suspension geometry changes easier.

The 1969 models were the most powerful road cars Porsche had yet produced. Even the more luxurious 911E could

The basic 911T interior was devoid of any additional features, yet was not too different from the more luxurious 911L and 911S in appearance. *Porsche AG*

This promotional shot from 1974 featured the 911S in Coupe and Targa versions. The attention-grabbing layout was to show off the new front and rear bumper designs necessary to meet by U.S. safety standards. This marked the beginning of the 911's second decade and the first major change in body styling. Unlike most European auto makers attempting to comply with U.S. crash bumper standards, Porsche managed to handsomely integrate the 5-mile-per-hour buffers into the car's design. *Porsche AG*

top 130 miles per hour and clock 0 to 60 in an average of 8.4 seconds. Speeds that had previously been the domain of the 911S, which was now even faster. With improvements in suspension, performance, and increased horsepower, 1969 became a watershed year for Porsche.

While the 911S was the best model you could buy, it wasn't necessarily the best Porsche for the money. That distinction, oddly enough, fell on the lowest-priced model, the 911T. In creating an entry level 911, Porsche eliminated a lot of interior trim features, used lighter weight carpet, and so on, basically creating a stripped-down version. That also translated into lighter overall weight, and as a result, the 110-brake horsepower 911T, equipped with the optional five-speed gearbox, could accelerate to 60 in 8.1 seconds and reach a top speed of 129 miles per hour. Nearly a match for the more expensive 140-brake horsepower 911E. The savings between the two models was $1,200. Not exactly chump change in 1969. The lighter weight 911T was also ideal for club racing. Works driver Vic Elford had even used a 911T (equipped with an S engine) to score his Monte Carlo Rallye victory.

The 911 was revised again in 1970 with the "C" Series, equipped with a larger displacement engine, 2,165 cc, and minor

The demands of competition finally brought about an entirely new breed of 911 in the 1973 model year, the RS 2.7. The car was offered in Sport or Touring versions (pictured). The RS 2.7 in Touring configuration featured opening rear quarter windows, reclining Recaro front seats, and folding rear +2 seats. A rear window wiper, power windows, and even a sunroof could be ordered as options.

suspension changes to further improve steering response. The 911 became exclusive this year, as the 912 was discontinued and replaced by the VW-Porsche 914 midengine model. The 911T now delivered 125 brake horsepower, the 911E 155 brake horsepower, and the 911S 180 brake horsepower, with a top speed in excess of 140 miles per hour.

By model year 1972, output was at an all-time high for the 911 with the E and S having gained 10 brake horsepower and the T an additional 5 brake horsepower. The 1972 models were also distinguished by being the first equipped with an aerodynamic chin spoiler under the front bumper. Porsche engineers determined that the spoiler reduced front end lift at 140 miles per hour. Not exactly the average driving speed, but there were still those who took their cars into competition.

As for Porsche, competition was, as it had been since the 1950s, a major factor in the evolution of their cars, and as the 1972 racing season came to an end, so too did an era in Porsche history. Things around Zuffenhausen were about to change.

Somewhere between the road and track, the Sport version of the RS 2.7, known as the "lightweight," was an out-of-the-box race car that could also be driven on the street. Like the Touring, the cars were distinguished by a special body design and the not-so-subtle Carrera name scrolled along the side of the car.

By 1974 Porsche was building cars that could be taken right into competition. This Carrera RS 3.0 is the actual factory test car driven by Jürgen Barth.

CHAPTER THREE

RENNSPORT

Carrera RS 2.7, Carrera RS 2.8, Carrera RS 3.0, and RSR

Many consider the Carrera RS 2.7 to be the definitive 911. The example pictured is an original factory-built M471 "Lightweight" Coupe. Serial number 911 3600284, it was completed on December 1, 1972. It is painted in the most popular color for the 1973 Carreras—Grand Prix White with blue trim and matching Fuchs wheels. The GPW cars were also available with red or green script and color-matched wheels. Nine other standard colors and 15 special colors at extra cost were available, as well as matches to sample colors.

The interior of the M471 was bare bones to eliminate as much weight as possible. The instrument cluster had only four gauges, the racing seats were covered in lightweight black cloth, most of the soundproofing was removed, and the regular carpet was replaced with lightweight black needle felt. The doors were covered with flat panels and a simple pull strap was used to operate the latch. The roll cage added weight back into the equation but was offset by eliminating unnecessary equipment like the passenger side sun visor, glovebox, rear seats, and trim.

Nothing quite equals the sensation of being pressed back hard into the driver's seat when you shift gears. It is the same sensation you feel just as a commercial jet lifts off—a firm, linear g-force that has speed written all over it. For the fortunate few who purchased the 911 Carrera RS 2.7 in 1973, this was the feeling that awaited them. Here was the road-going Porsche at its absolute best, a car developed for competition—an air-cooled six that was capable of taking on Ferrari's 12-cylinder Daytona and De Tomaso's V-8 Ford-engined Panteras in the GT competition.

The need for a car like the RS 2.7 was, in many ways, the result of the aforementioned Italian makes, which were threatening to win the GT class by sheer brute power over the 911's more agile handling. The 2.4-liter 911S was in need of a competitive edge, and Zuffenhausen's creation of the Carrera Renn Sport 2.7 was that edge honed to perfection.

In 1972, the 911S was being punished for breaking the laws of physics—the original body designed by Butzi Porsche having finally reached aerodynamic limits that the improved powertrain and suspension were capable of exceeding. With the 911S approaching speeds of 150 miles per hour, drivers experienced lift at the rear, resulting in less-than-desirable oversteer through fast corners. The RS 2.7 then, was a carefully engineered redress—a lighter, more powerful, better balanced, and more aerodynamic version of the 911S.

The fundamentals of the RS had already been established in 1967 by Ferdinand Piëch's experimental department at Weissach with the 911R. Powered by an engine derived from the Carrera 6, the 911 body was made lighter and fitted with fiberglass front fenders, doors, deck lids, and bumpers. Piëch's department built 3 prototypes, and another 20 were assembled at Zuffenhausen and fitted with steel bodies manufactured for Porsche by the Karl Baur company of Stuttgart. The cars, equipped with 911S shocks

and antiroll bars, 901/22 engines with Weber 46IDA3C1 triple-throat carburetors, and Nürburgring (competition) gear ratios, were painted white and had stripped interiors and Scheel bucket seats. They were used by the works team and some were sold to select private owners. That was as far as the 911R project went in 1967. A proposal to build 500 for homologation as Grand Touring cars never got past the sales department, which determined that 40 cars a month would have to be sold to reach the required sales figures necessary for homologation. Obviously they had never spoken to Enzo Ferrari!

Five years later, following the appointment of Dr. Ernst Fuhrmann as chairman of the Porsche executive committee in March 1972, the decision was finally made to develop a racing-type 911. As Porsche's technical director in 1971, Fuhrmann realized that the time had come to take advantage of Porsche's experience in Can-Am racing and translate that to the 911. "At the moment," said Fuhrmann in 1972, "we are ready to harvest the fruits of those years with the 908 and 917." The first car to be developed was the 1972 Carrera RS 2.7, essentially a refined version of Piëch's 1967 911R.

As with the 911R, mass was again the first factor to be addressed. Every part of the 911 was attacked to reduce the homologated weight of the RS. The Carrera body was lightened with the use of thinner-than-standard sheet steel measuring 0.70 millimeters (the usual was from 1.00 to 1.25 millimeters) for the doors, roof, luggage compartment lid, front fenders, luggage compartment floor, rear seat recess in the floor pan, even the shift lever platform! Weight reduction was also achieved through the use of lighter Belgian-made Glaverbel-laminated safety glass all around. Another 7.7 pounds was shaved with the use of Bilstein shock absorbers, marking the first time that the German-made gas-pressurized shocks would come as standard equipment.

Production of the Carrera RS 2.7 began in October 1972. This is one of the prototypes built sometime during July and photographed during road tests in August. Nearly a third of the early cars built were M471 Sport or "Lightweight" models. *Porsche AG*

Every conceivable facet of the Carrera's construction was scrutinizd for ways to reduce weight; much of it was achieved in small increments, beginning with the interior. Most of the soundproofing was removed, and the regular carpet was replaced with lightweight black needle felt. Interior trim was cut down to only the essentials, and even they were simplified—flat door panels with a leather strap to operate the latches and a small plastic handle to pull the doors closed. These were ex-Fiat 500 parts. The dashboard was the standard 911 design, but with only essential instruments, no clock. The interior was stripped of every nonessential item. There was not so much as a passenger-side sun visor. No glovebox door. The rear +2 seats were absent, and thinly padded buckets with adjustable head restraints,

The *Bürzel*, or "duck's tail" spoiler, greatly reduced aerodynamic lift at high speeds, helping to reduce oversteer. It also added 2 miles per hour to the car's top end, which was now a lively 153 miles per hour in the Lightweight version.

The 2.7-liter engine was so extensively modified from the 911S 2.4 liter as to be virtually new. The RS 2.7 was bored out 6 millimeters to 90 millimeters, and the increase in swept volume combined with a higher compression ratio, different carburetion, and performance tuning delivered 210 brake horsepower at 6,300 rpm.

Sport and Touring versions of the RS 2.7 were available from the Porsche factory in 1973. The sport model, in front, is equipped with a roll cage, battery cut-off switches (on cowl), and the rubber quick-release clamps on the front decklid.

rolled edges, and lightweight black cloth upholstery replaced the Recaro driver and passenger seats in the 911S. Also missing from the Carrera RS were undercoating, doorsill trim, coat hooks, and springs to counterbalance the front deck lid.

From the outside, the Carrera RS 2.7 was distinctively identified with "C A R R E R A" script running the length of the sills between the wheel openings, and a *Bürzel* (German for "duck's tail") fiberglass rear deck lid. This was fitted with rubber quick-release clamps, again to cut down on weight. The real advantage, however, was the greatly reduced aerodynamic lift provided by the spoiler, which not only reduced the 911's oversteer problem but added 2 miles per hour to the car's top end—a lively 153 miles per hour. An incidental effect was that it also raised the pressure at the grille, admitting air to the engine room, thus increasing airflow to the engine compartment and lowering oil temperatures.

As with the 1967 911R, fiberglass (polyester) was used for both the front and rear bumpers to reduce weight. Larger rear wheel arches on the Carrera also permitted 7-inch rims to be used in combination with the standard 6-inch fronts. The extended fenders widened the base from which 2 more inches at each side could be added on under the provisions of the GT regulations. The track was 54.0 inches at the front and 54.9 inches at the rear. Porsche was now able to fit Fuchs 15-inch forged aluminum alloy "S" pattern wheels on the 2.7, with either Pirelli Cinturato CN36 or Dunlop SP D4 tires, sized 185/70x15 for the front with lower profile 215/60x15s at the rear. The antiroll bars were also much stiffer, increased in diameter from the standard 15 millimeters to 18 millimeters in front and 19 millimeters at the rear. As a result, the RS 2.7 could now corner at the highest lateral g-force of any production Porsche: 0.912. None of the others could break the 0.9 g barrier.

Under the fiberglass deck lid was the improved Carrera six-cylinder engine. Since it was larger than 2.5 liters in size, FIA rules allowed displacement to be increased to the next class

Performance handsomely packaged. The Carrera RS 2.7 Touring was essentially a 911S interior with the 2.7-liter engine, suspension, and body. The front end was fitted with a prominent air dam below the front bumper and, in this case, optional driving lights. The design allowed for placement of a European number plate. The area could also be cut open as an air intake, which was usually the case on racing versions, although this was more common on the later RS 3.0 and RSR variants. *Autocar* tested a 2.7 Touring in 1973 and reported a time of 5.5 seconds from rest to 60 miles per hour, the quarter mile in 14.1, to 100 miles per hour in another nine-tenths and a top speed of 149 miles per hour. For 1973, this was the ultimate street car, the six-cylinder tormentor of Ferrari, Pantera, and Corvette.

The RS 2.7-liter engine was a more powerful version of the 2.4-liter 911S motor. The increased swept volume of the boxer engine raised brake horsepower from 190 at 6,500 rpm to 210 at 6,300 rpm.

size, which was 3.0 liters. The Carrera had the same stroke as the 2.4-liter Porsche sixes, 70.4 millimeters, but a larger bore, up from 84.0 millimeters to 90.0 millimeters. This was the largest bore ever used on a 911 engine to that time, and it gave the RS the same piston size and rod length as the 5.4-liter 12 used in the 917/10. The six's displacement became half that of the 12, 2,687 cc, or in marketing terminology, 2.7 liters.

The RS engine, designated as the Type 911/83, was essentially much like the 911S that preceded it. The compression ratio was identical, 8.5:1, and the 2.7 used the same Bosch mechanical injection, valve sizes, and timing as the 2.4-liter 911S. Output was 210 brake horsepower at 6,300 rpm (an increase of 20 brake horsepower over the "S"), although the engine could easily be pushed well beyond, with

The interior of the Carrera RS 2.7 Touring was almost identical to that of the 911S with the exception of the Recaro seats and the steering wheel. The Touring could be ordered with an AM/FM radio and even a power sunroof.

the rev limiter set at 7,300 rpm, maximum torque was rated at 188 lb-ft at 5,100 rpm, and all this was achieved on regular octane fuel! Drive was carried through a 915 five-speed transaxle as used in the 911S, but with fourth and fifth ratios raised slightly. Porsche claimed acceleration times of 5.8 seconds to 60 miles per hour.

Although not publicly introduced until the Paris Motor Show in October 1972, Porsche started marketing the Carrera RS 2.7 privately to prospective customers months before, in the hopes of bolstering orders to expedite the car's homologation in Group 4. Following *Fédération Internationale de l'Automobile* rules, Porsche had to build 500 examples to get FIA sanction. As it turned out, reaction to the Carrera was beyond Porsche's greatest expectations. It presold 51 cars before the Paris debut and within a week after the show closed had firm orders for the remaining 449 cars! The year's supply was sold out in a matter of weeks. On November 27, 1972, the FIA granted Porsche Homologation number 637 for Appendix J, Group 4. Overwhelmed by stunning sales, Porsche decided to build another 500, and when those were sold out by the following April, the factory turned out a third batch. When production of the Carrera RS 2.7 concluded, 1,583 had been built, including the original homologation cars, giving Porsche a double *fait accompli*. Not only had Zuffenhausen exceeded its sales goal by better than three times, the Carrera RS 2.7 could now be homologated in the Group 3 Grand Touring category as well!

Three versions of the RS 2.7 were produced. The Touring model, M472, incorporated 911S features including carpet, more soundproofing, opening rear windows, reclining Recaro front

Competing in Group 5, the Porsche Carrera RSR 2.8 of Peter Gregg and Hurley Haywood at Daytona in 1973. The car finished first and repeated its performance at Sebring.

The next evolution of the Carrera was the 230-brake horsepower RS 3.0 of 1974. The example pictured is one of the rarest of the 3.0 models, as it was the Porsche factory's test car. It was driven by Jürgen Barth, a second-generation mechanic and race driver working in the Porsche Sports Department. His father, Edgar Barth, had driven for Porsche at Le Mans in 1962, finishing first in class and seventh overall with Hans Herrmann in the number 1018 Carrera GTL. A decade later in the 1971 24 Heures du Mans, Jürgen Barth and co-driver René Mazzia finished eighth overall in a 911S. Barth went on to become Porsche's Safari team manager and one of the factory's top drivers.

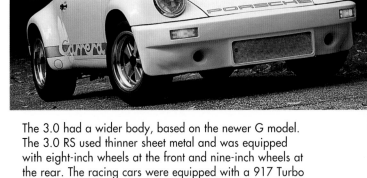

The 3.0 had a wider body, based on the newer G model. The 3.0 RS used thinner sheet metal and was equipped with eight-inch wheels at the front and nine-inch wheels at the rear. The racing cars were equipped with a 917 Turbo braking system to scrub off the speed generated by the full-race version of the 3.0, which delivered 330 horsepower.

NEXT
Chassis number 911 460 9040 is one of only 37 built in 1974. This was the factory works car driven by John Fitzpatrick to the 1974 FIA Cup for GT cars and to a first in class and fifth overall finish at Le Mans in 1975. The RSR 3.0s produced by the Competition Department were built directly to racing specifications for Group 4, Special Grand Touring. The GEORG LOOS name across the top of the windshield was a common sight on factory works cars. One of the better "give-and-take" relationships in European motorsports, Loos was one of Porsche's biggest customers. In return for maintaining his private team of cars, Loos helped sponsor the Porsche factory's racing effort. After the 1975 season, the car was retired and remained at the Porsche factory until 1982. Approximately 20 of the original cars are still in existence.

Designated 911/72, the RSR engine was entirely new, displacing 2,806 cc and developing 308 brake horsepower at 8,000 rpm. At the time, this was the "busiest" looking engine to come from the racing department.

seats, and folding rear +2 seats. A rear window wiper, power windows, and even a sunroof could be ordered as options. Outside, the cars looked almost identical; however, the Touring had steel bumpers. The M472 carried two 6-volt batteries, one on either side of the spare tire, while the M471, the RS *mit Sportausstattung* (with sport equipment) employed a single 12-volt battery located on the left side. A total of 200 Sport (lightweight) cars and 1,308 RS Touring were built during RS 2.7 production.

The Lightweight, although intended for club racing and amateur motorsports, could also be driven on the street, but with a great sacrifice of comfort and lack of convenience in the bargain. Wrote race driver and motor journalist Paul Frére of the 2.7 Sport model, "If you drive at city traffic speeds on a rough road, you may wonder if there are any springs fitted. . . ."

In either form, the Carrera RS 2.7 was a formidable car. The Touring version, weighing 2,398 pounds, some 250 more than the Sport, and a second slower off the line to 60, was still capable of reaching nearly 150 miles per hour. In competition, the Lightweight Carrera 2.7 RS was faster and more agile, but the real competitor was the third version, the M491. Completed to

order at Porsche's Werk I, this became the factory's full racing model, known as the Carrera RSR or *Rennausstattung*. (In German you just keep adding letters until you get the word you want.)

The name Carrera itself was used by Porsche to denote high-performance models after the introduction of the 356A four-cam in the fall of 1955. The literal translation of *Carrera* means *race* and is taken from the Carrera PanAmericana Mexican road races held in the early 1950s. In 1953 and 1954, Porsche 550 Spyders won the 1,500-cc class, in what many considered at the time, along with the Mille Miglia in Italy, the toughest road race in the world. The back-to-back victories in Mexico forever linked the Carrera name with Porsche. "This isn't like driving a regular 911, or even a 911 RS," says former race driver Bruce Canepa. "When you get on the RSR, it nails you right into the seat." The car also nailed most of its competitors for two consecutive seasons. The Carrera RSR 3.0 that Canepa owns today was the factory works cars campaigned by John Fitzpatrick, Toine Hezemans, and Gijs van Lennep in 1974 and 1975. Supported by the Porsche factory and sponsored by Gelo (Georg Loos Racing), the car was driven by Fitzpatrick to the

On Mark Donohue's advice, Roger Penske ordered 15 Carreras to use for the 1974 International Race of Champions (IROC). The cars were a hybrid of RS and RSR, built to look more like production 911s. The cars had flared rear fenders and a similar front end to the RSR, as well as the duck's tail decklid. A dozen of the cars are seen here at the Porsche factory late in 1973, before being shipped to the United States. *Porsche AG*

FIA GT Cup title in 1974, to class victories at Spa, the Nürburgring, Dijon, the Norisring, Imola, and to a stunning first-in-class and fifth overall finish at Le Mans in 1975.

The 1974 Carrera 3.0 RSR can best be defined as an evolutionary car in that its design and engineering evolved over a number of years, through the advancement of RS and RSR types, rooted as far back as the 911R, and progressing through the 2.7-liter RS and 2.8-liter RSR series.

The 1974 Carrera 3.0 RSR competition cars—in essence full-race versions of the limited-production 3.0 RS models—were assembled by the Porsche Competition Department and sold as ready to race. For 1974, the factory produced the Carrera 3.0 RS models which were homologated in Group 3 as an "evolution" of the Group 3

Loaded up and on their way to the dock, the first 8 of 15 Porsches built for the 1974 IROC Series. *Porsche AG*

Carrera RS 2.7. The Type 911 3.0 RSRs produced by the Competition Department were built directly to racing specifications for competition in Group 4, Special Grand Touring.

The conversion from 3.0 RS to RSR was made easier by the fact that the RS was almost a fully race-prepped car itself, equipped with the racing crankshaft, the very costly Type 917 brakes with four-piston calipers and 300-millimeter (11.8-inch) diameter perforated and ventilated discs, and twin master cylinders—17-millimeter diameter for the front brakes and 22-millimeter for the rear ones—providing an adjustment for front/rear pressure ratio. The five-speed transmission had an 80 percent limited slip differential and an oil pump, complete with cooling

Having had a stunning season in Porsche's 917/30, winning at Watkins Glen, Mid-Ohio, Edmonton, Laguna-Seca, and Riverside, in 1974 Mark Donohue drove a 911 RS Carrera in the International Race of Champions (IROC) series. At the end of the four-race 1974 season, it was Donohue (shown leading Peter Revson) who won the IROC title, besting a field that included Emerson Fittipaldi, Denis Hulme, A. J. Foyt, George Follmer, Peter Revson, David Pearson, Bobby Allison, Richard Petty, Bobby Unser, Roger McCluskey, and Gordon Johncock.

The wider fenders gave the RSR 3.0 its aggressive look. At the rear they were blended into the body but punctured at both their leading and trailing surfaces by air vents to cool the rear brakes. The wider front fenders were smoothly faired into the nose panel, but at their rear edges—just at the door cut—they simply stopped, leaving a huge rear-facing opening. This break with convention looked and was so functional that it was immediately adopted by other builders of modified production cars.

This was the very last RSR built by the factory, serial number 0006X. In February 1976 former Porsche mechanic and race driver Ludwig Heimrath destroyed his RSR at Daytona and asked that the factory build him another. By this time Porsche was producing the 934, but Heimrath did not want a Turbo. Out of necessity and desirability, this final RSR did, however, incorporate most of the new 934 improvements to body and suspension design, but with the 3.0-liter, 355-horsepower motor. With this car, Heimrath won the Mosport 1,000-kilometer IMSA race in 1976. IMSA rewrote the rules for 1977 so that the RSRs could continue to compete effectively now in the GTO class, and Heimrath campaigned the car for another year. The unusual chassis number of the RSR denotes that it was built as an experimental car and out of serial number sequence.

Porsche supplied all the essentials in the cockpit of the Carrera RSR: a Recaro racing bucket seat, full harness restraint, roll bar, and a fire-extinguishing system. The interior was black and devoid of trim. The door panels had no armrests, and leather straps were used to close the doors and operate the lock. The driver faced a 10,000-rpm tach and a 300-kilometer-per-hour speedometer.

The 1974 RS Carreras converted to RSR versions for Group 4 competition were the most aggressive 911s yet conceived. For racing, the Type 911/77 engine of the 1974 Carrera RS was converted to the Type 911/75 of the RSR. The engines had aluminum pistons, cylinders, and cylinder heads, higher lift camshafts, slide throttles, and a breakerless capacity discharge twin-ignition system. Having a bore and stroke of 95 millimeters (3.75 inches) x 70.4 millimeters (2.8 inches), displacement was 2,992 cc. The compression ratio on RSR-tuned engines was raised to 10.3:1. With an output of 320 brake horsepower and uncanny handling at speed, they were the dominating cars in their class for two consecutive years.

The RSRs were equipped with center lock hubs carrying racing pattern wheels of 10.5-inch front and 14-inch rear width.

serpentine in the right front fender and a large, front-mounted engine oil cooler.

The RSR modifications mainly involved bringing the engine up to racing specification, fitting a sintered metal-lined clutch disc, widening the front and rear fenders to fit the wide magnesium racing wheels and changing the front suspension struts to provide a lower ride height.

For racing, the Type 911/77 engine of the 1974 Carrera RS was converted to the Type 911/75 of the RSR—a full 3-liter racing engine identical to the 1973 factory prototypes, which had been the first Porsche sixes to achieve the magic 300-horsepower mark. (This seems remarkable today when you consider that the 1997 Turbo S delivers 425 brake horsepower, and it is a production street car.) RSR engines had aluminum pistons, cylinders, and cylinder heads, higher lift camshafts, slide throttles, and a breakerless capacity discharge twin ignition system. Having a bore and stroke of 95 millimeters (3.75 inches) x 70.4 millimeters (2.8 inches), displacement was 2,992 cc. The compression ratio on RSR-tuned engines was raised to 10.3:1. Output was nominally 320 brake horsepower at 8,000 rpm, but ranged 10 horsepower above and below that, depending upon the individual engines.

The Competition Department supplied all the essentials in the stripped-down racing cockpit of the Carrera. The interior was furnished with a special Recaro racing seat with a high squab and headrest, full harness restraint, built-in roll bar, and a fire-extinguishing system. The driver faced a stock 911-style instrument panel equipped with a 10,000-rpm tach and a 300-kilometer-per-hour speedometer.

The cars were fitted with center-lock hubs carrying racing pattern wheels of 10.5- and 14-inch front and rear widths covered by almost comic book-proportion fenders made of fiberglass.

The overwide fenders gave the RSR 3.0 an incredibly aggressive stance. At the rear, the flares were blended into the body but punctured at both their leading and trailing surfaces by air vents to cool the rear brakes. The wider front fenders were smoothly flared into the nose panels, but at their rear edges, just at the door cut line, they simply stopped, leaving a huge rear-facing opening to vent air. This break with conventional fender design was so functional it was immediately adopted by other builders of modified production cars.

The racing modifications—interior, engine, suspension, bodywork, wheels, and tires—added about $6,000 to the cost of the basic 1974 Carrera RS 3.0, which at $25,000 was already the highest priced Porsche 911 ever.

As for the stature of the Carrera RSR in the eyes of the racing community, Mark Donohue summed it up quite nicely after

The 2,893-cc, 355-horsepower RSR weighs 2,070 pounds. Because of the 934 suspension design, this 1976 RSR is slightly wider in the rear than earlier models.

testing an RSR prototype at the Paul Ricard Circuit in France. Said Donohue, who was never long on words, "The Carrera is, without a doubt, the very best off-the-shelf production race car available at any price."

On Donohue's advice, Roger Penske ordered 15 Carreras to use for the 1974 International Race of Champions (IROC). The cars were a hybrid of RS and RSR, built to look more like production 911s, thus more readily identifiable to spectators as Porsche road cars. Each was tested on the Weissach skid pad and tuned to give comparable performance before being shipped to Penske. All of the engines were set up to deliver around 316 brake horsepower. If there was any advantage a driver could gain in the IROC series, it was in knowing how to drive a 911. Ironically, at the end of the season, it was Donohue who won the IROC title, besting a field that included Emerson Fittipaldi, Denis Hulme, A. J. Foyt, George Follmer, Peter Revson, David Pearson, Bobby Allison, Richard Petty, Bobby Unser, Roger McCluskey, and Gordon Johncock. Not bad company.

The biggest winner of all was P O R S C H E, its name boldly spelled out on each of the brilliantly painted cars, seen by millions of motorsports fans on ABC's *Wide World of Sports*, which broadcast the final race in the series from Daytona. No amount of paid advertising could ever have equaled the exposure Porsche received from the IROC series.

Throughout Europe and all across America, the RS and RSR were almost unbeatable for two consecutive years, and even well into the late 1970s, the cars were still being campaigned successfully. From 1973 to 1976, Carrera RS and RSR models won titles in virtually every type of road race and hill climb championship held in the United States and Europe.

By the mid-1970s, racing technology was about to bring another change to the 911. The Carrera RS and RSR became the last factory competition cars equipped with normally aspirated engines. On the horizon was a new car, a new 911: the Turbo Carrera.

CHAPTER FOUR

TURBOCHARGED ROAD CARS

Porsche 930 and Turbos from 1975 to the Present

A year had passed before the turbocharged Model 930 made its way to the United States, and when the first cars arrived for sale they were badged as the 911 Turbo Carrera. At the time, $26,000 was the highest price ever asked for a production Porsche model in this country. In Europe the esteemed journal *Motor* wrote of the 930 Turbo in 1975, "We doubt there is any car in the world that is faster along a twisting road: there certainly isn't a car that gives more satisfaction when driven well. We've always admired Porsche for producing beautifully engineered machines. In the Turbo, they have the finest driving machine you can buy." This superbly restored example was redone by the Porsche factory.

For an additional $120, the Turbo Carrera could be ordered with the special T U R B O graphic that spread across the rear of the body—a none-to-subtle notice as to which car had just passed you!

Turbo-generated energy is free horsepower. That's a fairly generalized interpretation but basically true. A turbocharger works off wasted energy in the exhaust gas stream, which is used to spin the turbine. The turbine acts upon a shaft powering a compressor, which draws in air, compresses it, and then forces the air into the cylinders. Combined with a higher fuel-injection rate, specific output from an engine can be significantly increased. Better than doubled in some instances. That is the layman's explanation. It is a simple principle that has been around since Swiss engineer Alfred Büchi patented the turbocharger in 1905 to increase power output from diesel engines. The turbo's greatest automotive application, however, was racing. In the early 1970s, Porsche's 12-cylinder 917 Can-Am cars were unleashing 1,200 brake horsepower. And it was during this period that the formula was born for the Porsche 911 Turbo.

A road car with a turbocharged boxer engine could easily surpass the highest performance of the race-bred Carrera 3.0 RSR, which at its best was turning out 350 brake horsepower. Designing a turbocharged engine for the flat-six boxer motor, however, presented a multitude of problems, not the least of which was a means of regulating the boost pressure. This had not presented itself as an obstacle on the 917 Can-Am cars, on which the boost was always at the maximum. For a production road car, however, there would have to be a means of controlling boost pressure or there would be spent 911 engines in record numbers. Control was achieved with the addition of a wastegate, a device to divert exhaust gasses away from the turbine at a predetermined level, thus preventing boost pressure from going beyond a specific psi or atmosphere. For the first 911s the limit was 12 psi (0.8 atmosphere).

Porsche engineers also had to overcome turbo oiling problems and high temperatures that reached over 1,600 degrees Fahrenheit, but by 1973 they had sorted out all the technical problems and built the first turbocharged 911 Carrera RSR racing engines. A year later the turbo was ready for production, and the first model, the 930, made its debut in the fall at the Paris salon.

The car was first introduced to the European market as the 930 and a year later to America as the 911 Turbo Carrera, a car that Porsche fanatics were willing to mortgage their souls to Zuffenhausen to own. In 1976 the 911 Turbo sold for more than $26,000, making it the most expensive production 911 ever sold up to that time. And there were no discounts. Lots of waiting and little argument about color or options.

There was no mistaking the Turbo Carrera for any other 911 model. Most came with the word TURBO swept back over the flared rear fenders in letters 8 inches high, Perelli 215/60VR-15 tires, and Porsche's now famous "whale tail."

The 245-brake horsepower Turbo Carrera was more than another 911; it was what one magazine described as "the ultimate extension of the 911." In many ways, it was exactly that, the car Porsche's exclusive clientele had been asking for since the turbocharged RSR first appeared in competition. But God help the inexperienced driver who thought this was just another, faster, more costly 911.

When the Turbo first hit America, owners who were unfamiliar with the situation race drivers like to call "trailing throttle oversteer" found themselves destined for costly visits to the body shop. In any given corner, near or at the limit, the immediate instinct of an inexperienced driver was to back off the throttle, a serious error with the Turbo. This caused the back end to lift and the wheels to toe out, immediately inducing acute oversteer. Since the Turbo Carrera's basic power-on behavior was terminal understeer, once you were committed, the proper method was to stay on the throttle, correct with steering

In late 1974, Porsche launched the world's first production turbocharged sports car—the 1975 Porsche 911 Turbo. (Corvair enthusiasts may argue this point, but is the Corvair really a *sports* car?) This initial version featured a 3.0-liter, 245-horsepower flat-six turbocharged engine that propelled it from 0 to 100 kilometers per hour (62 miles per hour) in 5.5 seconds. *Porsche AG*

input, and let the car do what it was engineered to do. (This is more difficult in reality than it is to write about; however, the alternative was usually a lesson paid for by check.) The car's quirky handling characteristics, however, were predictable and, in the hands of an experienced driver, an attribute.

In designing the Turbo, the Weissach engineers had used a suspension more closely tied to that of the RSR than a production 911, and there were precious few owners who had the skills to take its full measure. Those who did reveled in the Turbo's race car-like performance. Those who did not, however, either drove with caution after scaring the bejeezus out of themselves, went to a driving school, and learned how to handle the car, or drove it until their luck ran out.

Off boost, the Turbo was less torquey than the 911S. The 3-liter's compression ratio was also reduced to 6.5:1, absolutely vital in the Turbo, as the fuel-air mixture was already entering the engine compressed. The exhaust-driven turbine wheel developed speeds of up to 90,000 rpm, precompressing air to a density of 11.4 psi, and attaining an air-fuel charge that was truly an automotive alchemist's dream.

Tucked beneath the whale tail was the most potent engine Porsche had yet put into the hands of its customers, a 3.0-liter sohc opposed six developing 234 to 245 horsepower at 5,500 rpm and 246 lb-ft of torque at 4,500 rpm. Equipped with Bosch K-Jetronic fuel injection and a Kühnle, Kopp and Kausch (KKK) turbocharger, the Carrera could clock 0 to 60 in 6.7 seconds, the quarter mile in 15.08 at 99.5 miles per hour, and reach a top speed of more than 150 miles per hour.

Unlike the cammy 911S models, there was no sudden surge of power when you put your foot down. At first it seemed

as though nothing was happening and then you were suddenly pressed into the seat, as the exhaust note changed from a husky rasp to a robust bellow and the car began to gather speed at an almost alarming rate. It was not the jolt owners had anticipated but rather a relentless application of power that continued up to the 6,950-rpm rev limit. The momentary lapse in throttle response was known as turbo lag, the time it takes the turbine to build speed, or "spool up," a popular term in automotive magazines. With a lower compression ratio and the inherent lag characteristics, the Turbo Carrera was only eight-tenths of a second faster than a normally aspirated 911 from 0 to 60. On the other hand, once it got rolling, it was nearly 10 miles per hour faster in the quarter mile.

Snicking the all-new type 930 four-speed (the 911S used the five-speed) through the gears was almost euphoric, as engine tone and speed increased with every shift. In a matter of 15 seconds you were at more than 100 miles per hour, and it was easy to get caught up in the Turbo's straight line acceleration, believing that when a turn came up you could handle it. If you were Peter Gregg or Hurley Haywood, sure, but most drivers exploring the car's limits discovered that their skills were somewhat less finely honed than an IMSA champion's. For most Turbo Carrera owners in 1976, it was a year of driving dangerously before they learned to either control the car or their enthusiasm.

For the 1976 model year (September 1975 to August 1976) Porsche produced a total of 1,201 Turbos, 519 of which were sold in the United States. For the 1977 model year 1,772 examples were built, with 716 destined for American garages. The

Turbo Carrera name was dropped following the introduction of the new 3.3-liter Turbo model in 1978.

A single turbocharger was installed in a Porsche 911-based race car for International Group 4 competition in 1974. This model, the Porsche 911 Carrera RSR Turbo, preceded the turbocharged Porsche 934 and 935 entries, which went on to prove the performance advantages of turbocharging by scoring hundreds of victories in the 1970s and early 1980s, including seven overall victories in the 24 Hours of Daytona and an overall victory in the Vingt-Quatre Heures du Mans.

In the mid-1970s, when the FIA began de-emphasizing prototype racing cars in favor of production-based machines, Porsche was ideally positioned to take advantage of the change.

As with many of its technical innovations, Porsche first developed twin-turbocharging for its racing programs—to be more specific, for its all-conquering Porsche 917/10 and 917/30 race cars created for the 1972–1973 SCCA Can-Am series. In 1974, a single turbocharger was installed in a Porsche 911-based race car for International Group 4 competition. This model, the Porsche 911 Carrera RSR Turbo, preceded the turbocharged Porsche 934 and 935 entries that went on to prove the performance advantages of turbocharging by scoring hundreds of victories in the 1970s and early 1980s, including seven overall victories in the 12 Hours of Daytona and one overall victory in the 24 Hours of Le Mans.

Despite their high state of tune, the turbocharged 934 and 935 race cars were fundamentally based on the road-going 911 tub and powertrain, making them eligible to compete in the World Championship of Makes. The 935 quickly became the dominant endurance racer of the decade, clinching the WCM

Aside from performance, the 1976 Turbo Carrera offered an interior befitting the car's lofty $26,000 price. Leather upholstery, power windows, Blapunkt AM/FM stereo with power antenna, air conditioning, auto heat control, tinted glass, heated outside mirror, headlight washers, fog lights, rear window wiper, and heavy-duty Bilstein shock absorbers were all standard equipment. The only options were the electric sunroof ($675), limited-slip differential ($345), heavy-duty starter ($50), and the T U R B O lettering ($120).

THE 934 AND 935

Porsche's 911-Based Turbocharged Race Cars

The 911 RSR Turbo was the first production-based model to be equipped with a turbocharged boxer engine, a prelude to the factory's full-blown assault on Group 4 and Group 5 racing in 1976. These were 930 Turbos modified for FIA competition, the "4" and "5" indicating the group for which each had been homologated. (There was also a midengine 936 Spyder for Group 6 competition, which had no requirements for production-based bodywork.)

The 934 qualified for Group 4, Grand Touring, by virtue of the production level achieved by the 930 Turbo (and 911 Turbo Carrera) and was essentially a production 930 modified at the factory for competition.

The 935 was a significantly modified 930, designed to compete in the Special Production Car category, which was open to modified cars from Group 1 through 4. As noted by Porsche historian Tobias Aichele, "The Types 934 and 935, developed in Weissach, were built in Zuffenhausen under the direction of Elmar Willrett. From the outset, the 934 was intended as a customer race car. The fact that the factory itself entered both 934 and 935 models in competition is due to a change in the rules, which were influenced by various international interests. Porsche adapted to the changes, prepared only one works 935 for the 1976 season [Karl Ludvigsen in *Excellence Was Expected* states that two 935 race cars were prepared by the factory for the 1976 season], and won the world championship for the fourth time, repeating its 1969, 1970, and 1971 successes but this time with production-based cars instead of a sports prototype."

While the 934 was close to a street car in appearance, very reminiscent of Carrera RS 2.7, the 935 was a rolling test bed for ever-improving technology. As Group 5 cars became ever more competitive, Porsche and Martini, Porsche's racing partner, began to modify the 935 until only the basic 911 silhouette remained.

The 935s virtually dominated GT racing throughout the late 1970s. The example pictured is campaigned today in vintage racing by Art Pilla of Ridgewood, New Jersey. The number 112 Golden Eagle car pictured is a 1980 935 K-3.

With the now famous 935 slant nose reshaping the 911's forward lines and spoilers towering above the rear deck lid, the cars gradually moved farther and farther from the 911 configuration until they were almost a parody of the production cars. They were also the inspiration for countless knockoffs, both in competition and for the street. Even Porsche contributed to the model's proliferation by offering kits that allowed the conversion from 934 to 934/5.

The 935 slant nose came about as the result of a variance in the FIA rules for Group 5. As noted in Ludvigsen's *Excellence Was Expected*, the rules stated, "The original outside shape of the bodywork should be retained," however, the rules also stated ". . . the material and shape of the wings (fenders) are free." Free meant that Porsche could redesign the fenders to improve the car's aerodynamics. Wrote Ludvigsen, "The Porsche engineers seized on the specific permission granted in the second sentence to cut off the tops of the fenders completely, headlights and all. This helped reduce aerodynamic drag and also improved visibility by reducing the area of the front of the car in profile. Vents in the fender surfaces relieved pressure in the wheel wells. The headlights were moved behind transparent covers in the front spoiler of the new nose, which cut 0.4 seconds from the best lap time at the Paul Ricard track."

Beneath the rear deck lid was the 2,808-cc Type 935 engine, packing water-cooled four-valve heads, intercooling (later adapted for the new 3.3-liter production 911 Turbos introduced in 1978) and an output variously rated from 590 net brake horsepower at 7,800 rpm to better than 600 brake horsepower. With a boost of 23 psi from the KKK turbocharger, usable only for short periods, output was rated as high as 630 brake horsepower.

In its final configuration, the 935 was the most powerful 911 derivative built up to that time. In competition trim, a 935 tested by *Road & Track* in 1976 turned 0 to 60 miles per hour in 3.3 seconds, the quarter mile in 8.9, and a top test speed of 150 miles per hour, achieved from a standing start in just 11 seconds! In 1979 a works 935 driven by Klaus Ludwig and the Whittington Brother brought Porsche an overall victory in the celebrated 24-hour marathon at Le Mans.

Even after Porsche ceased further development of the 935, privateer racers continued to win championship titles with factory-built cars (approximately 10 were sold to private teams), most notably Kremer, which also modified 930s into the 935 K3 and K4 models, both of which were put into limited production by the Kremer Brothers.

The reign of the 935 and 936 finally came to an end in 1981, after the rules were changed once again to move the sport away from production-based vehicles. But in the brief period from 1976 to 1980, the 935 had earned its place in the pantheon of great sports cars. Another legendary 911 model.

manufacturer's laurels every year from 1976 through 1980 and winning the more than 2,000-cc category in the last season of the series in 1981. With drivers such as Peter Gregg, Klaus Ludwig, John Fitzpatrick, Danny Ongais, George Follmer, Al Holbert, and Hurley Haywood taking these cars to repeated victories, Porsche's domination of GT racing was so absolute that at one time the question wasn't whether Porsche would win, but rather which Porsche would win.

With the 3.3 in 1978 came another advance in Porsche technology, the intercooler, which reduced intake air temperatures by

as much as 108 degrees Fahrenheit, allowing smaller turbochargers, higher boost pressures, and raising specific output to 300 brake horsepower.

A year after the 3.3's introduction it was withdrawn from the American market due to the energy crunch that began late in 1979, and it was a few years before the car was "officially" sold again in the United States. In Europe, the 3.3 remained in production as the 930, and "gray market" Turbos managed to keep a steady stream of cars on American roads despite import restrictions.

The temptation of the Turbo eventually led to another plea from consumers: the power of the 930 coupe in a Cabriolet and Targa version. The wisdom of putting so much power into an open car was questionable, but Porsche had almost always bowed to the wishes of the paying customer, and in 1986 both Targa and Cabriolet versions of the Turbo were introduced.

The factory's 930 and 935 *flachtbau* (flat nose) cars also attracted a great deal of attention over the years and these too became

The second production 911 Turbo was introduced in 1978. The addition of an intercooler and an increase in displacement to 3.3 liters raised power to 265 horsepower. *Porsche AG*

Topless Turbos were finally introduced in 1986 in response to customer demands for an open version. Although there was some concern at Porsche as to the wisdom of such a high-performance car as a Cabriolet or Targa, it was decided to build what the customers wanted. Both Turbo versions proved to be very popular, although production was always kept short of demand. *Porsche AG*

available at a price. By the early 1980s, aftermarket tuners became heavily involved with the manufacturing of 930 flat-nose conversions for production 911 Turbos, as well as for other 911 models. The most famous European models were those produced by Uwe Gemballa in the late 1980s. In 1987 Gemballa told the author that "we try to please the customer . . . find out what people like, what is the best design, what they want out of *their* car." The ultimate example of this Stuttgart tuner and coachbuilder's work was the 1987 Mirage, a totally modified 911 slant nose with Ferrari Testarossa-style body strakes, lowered roofline, a custom-built leather interior, and a Ruf Automobiles twin turbocharged engine. The cars sold for a staggering $300,000!

After more than a decade, the slant-nose Turbo is still one of the most popular 911 conversions in the world. Among the best known examples in the United States are those produced by Alan Johnson Racing and Bob Anziano. Johnson was a Porsche racer and dealer in southern California who had been campaigning 911s since 1967, the year in which his red C Production 911 coupe came out on top in the National Championship runoff at Daytona. Earlier in the year he had also placed ninth overall and first in the GT category at Sebring. Johnson won the SCCA C Production title again in 1968 and was a five-time National champion by the time he retired and opened his race shop in 1975. The Alan Johnson 930S Turbos are still regarded as among the best high-performance road cars ever built outside the Porsche factory.

Catering more to the aesthetic, rather than the performance-minded, Bob Anziano has created some of the most exotic 911 Turbo hybrids of the 1990s. Anziano is a custom coachbuilder in the tradition of the Porsche Special Works Department, where the only limitation is the size of your bank account. Bob Anziano also has a gift for imaginative designs, combining several different 911 models into one, such as a 1989 Speedster with a Turbo rear fender treatment, whale tail, and a 930 slant-nose front end. This has become one of Anziano's most celebrated designs and perhaps the best nonfactory body style ever produced.

While there have been many tailors to the 911 over the past decade, both in the United States and Europe, the Turbo in its factory form is still the most desirable. The car's lineage has continued almost uninterrupted for over 20 years, constantly improved upon by Porsche with each successive model. In 1989, the new 964 platform was introduced, along with the all-wheel-drive Carrera 4, giving the venerable 911 yet another new lease on life. The 964 program was an evolution of the 1987–1988 Porsche 959 all-wheel-drive turbo competition cars, of which only 300 examples were built.

In 1993 Porsche introduced the third-generation turbo motor, a 3.6-liter developing 355 brake horsepower at 5,500 rpm. The new engine not only increased horsepower but torque, up to 383 lb-ft at 4,200 rpm. Top speed was also raised to an adrenaline-pumping 174 miles per hour.

After 30 years of production, the 911 became one of the most abundant sports cars in the world for customizers like Bob Anziano, in Santa Ana, California, who began with simple updates and conversions to 930 flat-nose models. One of the most outstanding of Anziano's customs was the *flachtbau* Turbo Speedster, elegantly combining the Porsche factory's 930 slant nose, 911 Turbo, and 911 Speedster into one eye-catching sports car.

The 3.6 was improved throughout from its predecessor, equipped with larger brakes and new 18-inch wheels, derived from the Carrera Cup cars, which gave a clear view of the brilliant red four-piston aluminum brake calipers. Although the 3.6 was the best Turbo model Porsche had yet built, its time was to be limited, just one model year, from October 5, 1992, through the end of production in December 1993, at which time Porsche concluded manufacturing of all other 911 models to reinvent itself once again for the car's 30th anniversary in 1994.

Zuffenhausen celebrated the 911's third decade with the introduction of the Type 993 Carrera, an altogether different car, yet instantly recognizable as a 911. Remarked Butzi Porsche in 1994, "[The new Carrera] is an absolutely worthy and masterfully made successor to all previous 911s."

By 1996, the Turbo Carrera had become the very image of the sought-after but unobtainable (and illegal in the United States, except for racing) all-wheel-drive, turbocharged 959. The body lines were a little sweeter, rounded at the rear in an almost 928 theme, with the front taking on more of the angular crispness around the headlights and fenders characterized by the limited-production 959 competition cars.

With the fifth generation (Turbo generations are considered 1974, 1978, 1991, 1994, and 1996), the 911 Turbo has reached

LEFT
Further engine development resulted in a boost to 315 horsepower in the third-generation 911 Turbo in 1991. The next-generation 911 Turbo was the 1994 model (shown here). Based on a revised 3.6-liter engine, this version produced 355 horsepower and accelerated from 0 to 60 miles per hour in 4.7 seconds. *Porsche AG*

TOP
Former race driver turned Porsche dealer and tuner Alan Johnson produced his own slant-nose conversions in the late 1980s, and his were not fiberglass but all steel. The Alan Johnson 930 Turbos were among the fastest and best-looking nonfactory Porsches to hit the road.

The most desirable (and most difficult to get) color for the 1994 model year was Pearlessence, a silver-white metallic that turned heads a half-mile away. The Turbo Carrera was now equipped with the new 3.6-liter engine (introduced in 1993), developing 355 brake horsepower at 5,500 rpm and 383 foot-pounds of torque at 4,200 rpm. The 3.6 was equipped with larger brakes and new 18-inch wheels that gave a clear view of the brilliant red four-piston aluminum brake calipers. The Turbo Carrera 3.6 was the most powerful and, at 174 miles per hour, fastest production car Porsche had yet delivered into the hands of enthusiasts.

its highest level of development, with the 3.6-liter aluminum al-loy, boxer engine delivering 400 brake horsepower and 400 lb-ft of torque through a six-speed transaxle, with full-time all-wheel-drive, limited slip differential, and automatic brake differential (ABD) traction control. The 1997 Turbo S refines performance even further by increasing horsepower to 424, making this the most powerful road car ever offered by Porsche.

For 1998, the Turbo will once again briefly bow out of the model line (as it did in 1985 for the U.S. market and in 1990 in Germany), while Porsche prepares to launch the all-new 1999 Carreras, which will be the first 911s to use liq-uid-cooled engines. As for the Turbo, no doubt Porsche's next iteration will once more redefine the limits of road car performance.

The 911 series was revised in 1995, and for 1996 Porsche brought out the most advanced version of the Turbo to date. Key elements of the new model included exterior styling, redesigned rear suspension, ABS 5 antilock brakes, stronger body shell, and enhanced driver/passenger comfort levels and ergonomics. Added to this package were the all-wheel-drive (AWD) system from the Porsche 911 Carrera 4, further revised bodywork featuring the unmistakable fixed "Turbo-wing" rear spoiler, and extensive luxury equipment including leather interior, power seats, and 150-watt audio system.

LEFT
The 1996 Porsche 911 Turbo was inspired by the legendary Porsche 959, a vehicle acknowledged as one of the great cars of the 20th century. Introduced in 1985 as a limited-edition model offered for sale outside North America, the 959 incorporated a twin-turbocharged engine and all-wheel-drive system in a 911 chassis. This marriage of power and handling resulted in an exotic supercar capable of winning such grueling competition events as the Paris-Dakar Rallye. The 1996 Porsche 911 Turbo featured these same concepts in a less expensive production version designed to be driven daily on North American roads. The limited-edition 1997 Turbo S (pictured), priced at $150,000, took performance one step further with a 425-brake horsepower 3.6-liter engine, becoming the most powerful Porsche road car to date. *Dan Lyons*

Extensive testing protocols at the Porsche factory ensure that a single 911 design is suitable to meet the world's strictest emissions, safety, and noise regulations. This has been Porsche's policy since the early 1970s, when Zuffenhausen redesigned the 911 to meet U.S. bumper regulations. *Porsche AG*

Developing 400 horsepower and 400 foot-pounds of torque from its 3.6-liter, twin-turbocharged and intercooled, horizontally opposed, six-cylinder engine, the 1996 Porsche 911 Turbo was the most powerful production Porsche ever offered for sale on this continent. Capable of 0 to 60 in 4.4 seconds and a top track speed of 180 miles per hour, it set another new Porsche performance standard.

CHAPTER FIVE

TARGAS, CABRIOLETS, AND SPEEDSTERS

Open Cars for the Road

Generations apart, yet so much alike, a rare 1952 Porsche America Roadster and 1997 Carrera 2 Cabriolet leave more in their reflections than meets the eye. The sleek 993 body styling combined with all-wheel-drive and Porsche's latest 3.6-liter, 282-brake horsepower engine and six-speed manual gearbox, make the 1997–1998 Carrera 4 Cabriolet the most advanced open car in Porsche's history.

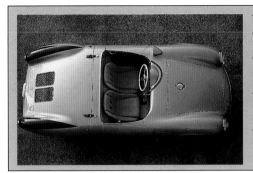

The open car has always been the cornerstone of the Porsche model line. Exotic models like the 550 Spyder established the Porsche legend in racing, while sporty Speedsters and luxury Cabriolets provided owners with a stunning variety of body styles from which to choose, along with several versions of Porsche coupes. It was thus inevitable that a successor to the 356 would have to follow along similar lines.

At the small Gmünd werke in the Malta valley, Dr. Ferdinand Porsche, his son Ferry Porsche, engineer Karl Rabe, and stylist Erwin Komenda began the design of a sports car to be built around Volkswagen components. The project was officially named the Type 356. The prototype body, assembled over a tubular space frame, was designed by Komenda and Ferry Porsche. Introduced in May 1948, the very first car to bear the Porsche name was a roadster. Although open cars became the cornerstone of the Porsche line, from the onset both open and closed versions of the 356 had been planned, and a decade later when Butzi Porsche was designing a car to replace the 356C, both coupe and cabriolet were under development. The 911, however, presented some interesting design challenges that the 356 had not. For one, the 356 had originally been an open car. The 911 was initially designed as a coupe. In automotive development, it is easier to put a top on a convertible than it is to remove the roof from a coupe.

The subject of a 901 cabriolet had been broached several times in the car's early development, and in the fall of 1962 three proposals were presented as one-tenth scale drawings and a scale model, which was sent to Wilhelm Karmann Company for a manufacturing feasibility study. Among the three proposals was one by Butzi Porsche that suggested a removable roof panel and folding rear window joined by a rigidly mounted roll bar. This was the least complicated means of creating an open 911 and also the least costly to manufacture.

By 1963, Porsche finances were spread pretty thin with production start-up for the 911 coupe and retooling for the new body at Reutter, which Porsche had been obliged to purchase. Building a cabriolet, which would require a partial redesign of the 911 and additional tooling costs, simply was not in the budget. Butzi's proposal was the perfect compromise, a car that could be both coupe and cabriolet and could be produced without substantial changes in the production line. The Targa became Porsche's first open top 911 model.

The car was described in a September 1965 press release as, ". . . neither a cabriolet nor a coupe, not a hardtop nor a sedan, but rather something completely new.

"With this model, we not only present a new car, but a new idea: the application of a safety hoop in a production car and thereby the world's first safety cabriolet. . . . It is Porsche's privilege to be the first auto manufacturer in the world to offer a roll bar on a production car. . . ."

In its presentation of the car, Porsche described the 911 Targa as having four top configurations: Targa Spyder, with the top removed and rear window folded; Targa Bel Air, with the top panel removed and rear window raised; Targa Voyage, with the roof in place and rear window lowered; and Targa Hardtop, with roof and rear window closed. While it was a bit contrived, there really were four different ways to arrange the top and rear window, each giving the car a distinctively different appearance.

Although the Targa was first shown in September 1965, it was only in prototype form and did not become available for sale until January 1967. During the ensuing months between the car's debut and production, Porsche engineers increased the integrity of the Targa bar for rollover protection and completed improvements in the removable top section. When the Targa finally arrived in showrooms, it was offered in three versions, 911, 911S, and as an option for the lower-priced four-cylinder 912.

The Targa model followed 911 evolution throughout the 1960s and in 1968 was featured for the first time with an optional solid glass rear window, which became standard the following year making the soft window an option. With the rear glass window and embedded heating elements to defrost the

The 911 Targa remained one of Porsche's most successful models from the time it first went on sale in January 1967 until the last cars were produced for the 1993 model year. The cars pictured are a 1976 (below) and a 1990 Targa Carrera, equipped with the 3.6-liter engine. Note the raised rear wing on the Carrera, which is automatically activated at speeds above 48 miles per hour. *Porsche AG*

backlight in winter, the 911 Targa became even more popular, and in 1970 accounted for more than 40 percent of all 911 sales. The Targa remained in production through 1993. In 1995, the new 993 series was introduced and the following year came a stunning and innovative new Targa design.

It seems that benchmark designs have become a habit with Porsche, and the 1996 through 1998 911 Targas illustrate the epitome of everything Porsche has stood for over the past 50 years. The new Targa is the most appealing and practical car since the 911 was introduced in 1964.

Targa not only represents a historic name for Porsche, but in this latest iteration, a monumental breakthrough in design evolution: the best aspects of a coupe and convertible without the compromises of either. There is no longer a panel to remove and store when you want the sun to shine in your face and the breeze to flow over the windshield. The touch of a button activates an electronic retractable glass roof panel that slides back under the rear window to provide the same open overhead view as did the original Targa with the roof panel removed. When the tinted glass roof is closed, additional protection from the sun is provided by an electronic retractable shade concealed within the windshield header that slides out to cover the roof panel, thus giving the appearance of a traditional cloth headliner.

Combined with the 282-brake horsepower 3.6-liter engine and Tiptronic transmission, Porsche created an amazing sports car that is suitable for every driving situation, be it the daily traffic grind or a wistful weekend road trip down some open, twisty section of highway.

While the Targa provided Porsche with a solution to a problem, it still had not addressed the need for a traditional Cabriolet. This, however, was the one model Porsche did not rush to produce, waiting 18 years before introducing a 911 convertible in 1983.

The lines of the 964 series were still very much like those of the earlier cars, with the exception of bumpers, headlights, and taillights. The Carrera script made famous by the RS 2.7 back in 1973 was optional on any Carrera model after 1989.

It was the end of an era in 911 history when Porsche discontinued the Targa Carrera after the 1993 model year. The example pictured is one of the last built in the 964 series.

The Cabriolet was not entirely a Porsche design, at least not from the windshield up. The patented convertible top was designed for Porsche by Gerhard Schröder. Rather than a conventional folding top design, the Cabriolet used a unique series of stamped steel panels—one in front and one in back—connected by the folding mechanism. The steel panels provided a solid surface upon which to attach the convertible fabric, significantly reduced wind noise, and in the process, offered some rollover protection with the top raised.

The first models had manually operated tops, but Porsche and Schröder were already at work on a fully automatic top even before the first Cabriolet was introduced. The electric top

With the 964 series, the 911 interior was refined to a more luxurious level with the addition of a center console for controls, shifter, and hand brake. This interior of this 1993 Carrera Targa is upholstered in black leather with herringbone fabric inserts.

offered a simple transformation from open to closed, and vice versa, without any intervention from the driver aside from pressing a button. Electric motors released the header locks, activated 13 moving bows and the top frame, concealed within the padded headliner, and in a matter of 20 seconds the whole operation was complete. To everyone's surprise, the pressed-steel substructure of the convertible was so rigid in the closed position, that the 911 Cabriolet actually tested in the wind tunnel with a lower Cd (coefficient of drag) than the 911 Coupe!

Even though Porsche now had two open cars, both continued to sell, Targa enthusiasts remaining true to their favorite model, while others drawn by the allure of a true convertible Porsche flocked to the new Cabriolet, which could also be ordered with a removable hardtop, giving the car an almost identical profile to that of the 911 Coupe.

As the Targa and Cabriolet became increasingly popular, there arose yet another demand from Porsche buyers for turbocharged versions of both models. After some hesitation,

The 911 Cabriolet was first introduced in 1983. This is a factory photo of an early 911SC Cabriolet with 3.0-liter engine. *Porsche AG*

The 1992 Carrera 2 Cabriolet was offered with the widebody Turbo Look. *Porsche AG*

The all-wheel-drive Carrera 4 was introduced as a Cabriolet version in 1990. The Carrera 4 was the most technologically advanced road model in 911 history, even superior to the 959 because of the C4's advanced all-wheel-drive system. The C4 system used a central tube containing the driveshaft and a viscous clutch connecting the front and rear axle. The C4 was designed to retain more of the rear drive character of the standard 911, with the viscous clutch automatically distributing output torque between the front and rear axles as required. *Porsche AG*

73

The 1986 widebody Cabriolet had all of the 911 Turbo features except the engine—the cars were powered by a normally aspirated 3.2-liter six. The interior on this example is a special order done in champagne leather, including the dashboard, which at the time was almost impossible to get in any color but black. The car was specially fitted with polished Fuchs wheels and is painted midnight blue with a blue top, a rare color combination. Back in 1986 the 911 interior was still very basic, and the special order leather trim was what really set this car apart from the rest of the 1986 Cabriolets. The car is from the Kent Rawson collection.

Rakish body lines of the 993 series Porsche 911 complement the open-air styling of the latest Cabriolet model. *Porsche AG*

A factory photo of an early 1987 911 Speedster with standard width body. Later versions were offered with the widebody Turbo look. Note that the European version is badged as a Carrera. The cars were never badged as Speedsters, even though that was the model designation. *Porsche AG*

Two generations of Porsche Speedsters. The black Speedster pictured was purchased from the factory by film star Steve McQueen. An avid motorsports enthusiast and racer, McQueen campaigned the car around southern California in the late 1950s and early 1960s. Ordered in racing trim, the Speedster was fitted with the seldom-seen Rudge chrome knock-offs, offered as an option. The car is owned today by his son, actor Chad McQueen. Contrasting the original 356 Speedster is a 1989 911 Speedster.

Another European 911 Speedster, this example from 1988 with the wider Turbo body. In this unusual low-angle view, the height of the rear tonneau becomes more obvious. This was the most unusual aspect of the Speedster design and one of its distinguishing characteristics. *Porsche AG*

Aside from the noticeably different exterior features, the first series 911 Speedster was identical inside to the 911 Cabriolet, luxuriously appointed in leather and with all the modern conveniences, even air conditioning.

Porsche management decided that if customers wanted Turbo Cabriolets and Targas, then Porsche would build them, and beginning in 1986 the 3.3-liter Turbo was available as a Coupe, Targa, or Cabriolet. Porsche now had three significant cars on the road at once. All that was missing was a modern-day version of Porsche's most famous 356 model.

By fulfilling the final pleas of sports car enthusiasts, Porsche completed the circle, returning at last to the tradition of the 356 era with the addition of a 911 Speedster in 1987.

The thinking behind the new Speedster, intended by design to recapture the unique character of the original car, was to create a modern version without compromising the 911 in the process. As it turned out, there was just enough of the 356 in the new Speedster to set it well apart from any other 911. Like the original, the windshield was lower and more steeply raked, laid back 5 degrees farther than the standard 911's, and with the top up, the car had a very

trim profile, repeating the earlier Speedster's shallow stance. But this was no simple roadster reincarnate. Forget the lower windshield and unlined manual top; for all intents you were behind the wheel of an 1989 Cabriolet surrounded by Porsche's traditional 911 instrument panel, bottom-pivot pedals (a truly homogenous link to

RIGHT
THE 1997 Boxster represents the first of a new generation of Porsche models. The 2.5-liter horizontally opposed Boxster engine is the first six-cylinder Porsche production engine to be water cooled and equipped with four-valve technology. The new 1999 Porsche 911 model is largely based on the Boxster's advanced engineering and front end styling. The model pictured is specially equipped with German-built TechArt Automobildesign GmbH. 17-inch wheels, lower front spoiler, side skirts, and rear fender air ducts. The car was modified by TechArt's U.S. division, German Tech, Inc., in Largo, Florida.

For 1993 Porsche brought the 911 Speedster back as a Carrera 2. The cars were far more stylish than the earlier version and, equipped with the 3.6-liter engine, more powerful as well. *Porsche AG*

the original 1954 Speedster) and multi-adjustable, power-operated leather-faced seats. A Porsche 911 by any other name.

The Speedster of the 1950s was a tinny blithe spirit of a car with a leaky canvas top, flimsy side curtains, an unpredictable (better get ready for the turn before you get there) Volkswagen-derived suspension, and an engine that sounded as though it were about to burst at every shift. For its time, it was *Pur Sang*.

The most distinctive and telling clue to the 911 Speedster's identity, since the factory chose not to reissue the original car's stylized script, was the unique rear tonneau design. Arching over the back of the two-seater, the one-piece cover gave the appearance of dual head fairings, while completely concealing the convertible top mechanism. Hinged from the rear, the cover lifted and the top unfolded from beneath. As simple as this may sound, deploying the cloth or folding it back was best done seasonally, so say owners of early 911 Speedsters. The operation of the 911 Speedster top was a far cry from the original 356 ragtop, which required all of a few seconds to reach back and grab hold of the header bow, pulling the top up and securing it to the windshield frame with two simple latches. The reverse procedure took even less time, if you cared little for the condition of the plastic rear window. You simply unlatched the top and threw it back.

The 911 Speedsters were modern, high-performance cars equipped with the 3.2-liter, fuel-injected six, dropping 214 brake horsepower to the ground at 5,900 rpm through a five-speed manual. The 911s shot from 0 to 60 in a scant six seconds and could easily tease the 150 miles per hour mark. The 356 Speedster, with its flat-four engine, could only

In 1993 and 1994 Porsche produced a second generation of 911 Speedsters. The newer models were more dramatically styled and more colorful than the first 911 series. The 1993–1994 Speedsters featured color-keyed wheels, dashboards, interior trim, and seatbacks. *Porsche AG*

have achieved such heroic speeds if dropped from a very great height!

The 911 Speedsters featured Turbo-style fenders and used Turbo-based underpinnings with struts in front and trailing arms in the rear. And while still given to rude awakenings when driven into a turn out of shape, the 911 Speedster so far exceeded the limits of the 356 Speedster's swing-axle hind quarters, that no reasonable comparison can be drawn between the two. When you get right down to it, they are like distant cousins of noble parentage who have little more in common than name.

A limited-edition model, only 2,100 Speedsters were built before the car went out of production at the end of the 1989 model year. The Speedster's popularity vastly exceeded the production run, and for two years after, they were selling used for more than they sold new.

With the all-new 964 series on the road in 1990, plans were under way to revive the Speedster as a Carrera model. The third-generation Speedster made its debut at the Paris Salon in October 1992, and once again Porsche had a hit on its hands. Initially sold with only the standard narrow-body Carrera Cabriolet fenderlines, by midyear, the Carrera Speedsters were also being offered with the wide Turbo fenders, at an additional cost.

The 1993 Speedsters were vastly improved over the first series, with a more easily operated manual top, Carrera RS seat shells painted in body color, and leather upholstery specifically designed for the Speedster model. The new interiors also featured another unusual feature for Porsche: body-colored instrument panel accents, shift lever, and parking brake handle (all usually a Special Works Department order). The Carrera Speedster was again produced as a limited edition, this time totaling only 930 cars.

Two Carrera Speedster models were offered for a brief production run in the 1994 model year, the second version equipped with the new Tiptronic transmission. The two-seaters did not reappear in 1995, and the all-new 1997 Boxster has since taken its place as the "Porsche Speedster" for the next century.

The Targa's reprise came in 1996 with an all-new design featuring a glass roof panel that slid rearward under the backlight. With the sleek new 993 body lines, 3.6-liter engine, and Tiptronic gearbox, the new Targa became one of Porsche's most innovative models ever. *Porsche AG*

This could be the most popular Porsche 911 ever built. Only time will tell, but the 1996 through 1998 Targa has certainly rewritten the books on sports car design, with an electronically operated sliding glass roof replacing the removable Targa top. Combined with the Tiptronic S transmission, which offers either the convenience of an automatic transmission or driver-selectable manual gear change from the center console-mounted shifter or remote Formula One-style steering wheel gear selector, the Targa becomes the most versatile 911 ever built.

CHAPTER SIX

LIMITED EDITIONS

The Special Works Department and Commemorative 911 Models

The *Sonderwuncsh*, or Special Wishes Department, more commonly know as the Special Works, was organized by Rolf Sprenger to cater to the needs of customers desiring special versions of the 911. The Works produces cars in special colors, fabrics, and trim to sample, or a complete "special order" car can be built. The only limit is the customer's bank account. The estimated cost of this Special Works C4 Cabriolet is $50,000 above the base price of the car.

The interior, dashboard, and door caps of this *Sonderwuncsh* project were done in cashmere leather rather than the traditional black. The dashboard trim, steering wheel, and shifter were hand-finished rootwood, and the seats were made to order with plaid inserts. The center console was also custom fabricated. All of the interior trim was covered in leather, including the instrument bezels, air vents, and control knobs.

In recent years Porsche has paid tribute to its halcyon past by introducing 911 models with historically significant names like Speedster, Carrera, and America. And it is perhaps just that Porsche's present should be so closely tied to its past.

One of the most significant model names drawn from the 1950s was the America Roadster, which bowed in 1992 as a limited-edition 911 to commemorate the 40th anniversary of the original Americas brought into this country by Max Hoffman in 1952 and 1953.

A look back at the historic 356 model upon which the 1992 911 was based is particularly important since the original America is perhaps the least known of all early Porsches.

It followed on the heels of the first 356 coupes and cabriolets, which, through Hoffman's efforts, had found their way into the hands of would-be racers in 1950 and 1951. By the end of the 1951 season a small but enthusiastic body of Porsche owners was successfully campaigning 356 Pre-A models in production sports car classes. The following year Hoffman received the first of 15 America Roadsters that would go to privateer racers such as Briggs Cunningham, Richie Ginther, Phil Walters, John Bentley, Jack McAfee, and John and Josie von Neumann. The lightweight, aluminum-bodied racers were to become the legitimate forerunner of the famed 356 Speedster.

Production of the America was so limited—in total just 16 cars bodied for Porsche by Gläser of Weiden—that they were never formally catalogued by the factory and were totally unpublicized in Europe. The market for the America was chiefly the United States and specifically Hoffman, who would ultimately purchase all of the cars but one.

Today, the few remaining examples are considered among the rarest of all Porsches, even though historically Porsche barely acknowledged their existence until the commemorative America models were introduced.

Since the days of the 356, Porsche has maintained a simple tenet: Make no change for the sake of change alone. Even though there are model years, the 911 was never viewed by Porsche as an annual model. The 911 evolved as changes became necessary. Having been around for 35 years, the 911 became the basis for countless variations on a theme, as independent designers rework older examples of the 911, giving the cars a new and often *outre vogue* look. Independent designers and engineers working outside the company have made countless contributions to the 911's evolution. Some have been brilliant, such as the Anziano *flachtbau* cars, elegantly blending the Weissach 930 with the 1989 Speedster, while European performance engineering firms like Ruf and Racing Dynamics have turned out 500-horsepower tuned variants of the 911 engine. Others, like the Gemballa Porsches of the late 1980s, were exercises in extremes, designed to take the 911 places even Porsche never dreamed of going.

Not to be outdone, Porsche has its own special in-house design studio devoted exclusively to custom work. Known as the Special Works Department, it is essentially a company within the company that is known only to the few. It is managed by designers, engineers, mechanics, and craftsmen who have been with Porsche for years, even decades. The Special Works is capable of building engines, suspensions, even complete bodies. Traditionally the Works deals with customer requests for individual modifications on stock 911s, as well as handling restorations of more venerable Porsches, the construction of private race cars, and maintenance and preparation of Porsche aircraft engines.

Among the Works' most interesting projects in recent years was a special version of the 911 known as the America GS, created by Porsche's Chief Stylist Harm Lagaay at the request of an

This Special Works C4 Cabriolet has a custom exterior color and top fabric. The paint is Champagne Yellow, with Afrika Korps beige fabric for the Cabriolet top.

Engine modifications are also part of the Special Works Department; however, on this C4 Cabriolet, the 3.6-liter engine was left stock.

The 911 America GS Roadster is a work of art. One of the German workers who assembled the car referred to it as "automotive sculpture," and when the car was flown into the PDI center for Porsche Cars North America in North Charleston, South Carolina, it was accorded the attention and care one would give a crated masterpiece being shipped from the Louvre to New York's Metropolitan Museum of Art.

This uncommon reverence for the 911 was not for the car alone, but for the time and talent that went into its design and execution. If the result were described as exorbitant, it would still be an inadequate term. The America GS was as close to a coach-built automobile as one can get in contemporary times.

If you go back through Porsche history, limited production cars have not been uncommon. The America commemorative model of 1994, for example, was limited to only 250 cars.

The America GS started life as one of the 40th Anniversary cars, a normally aspirated 911 wide-body Cabriolet. The "GS" epithet comes from the old 356 Carrera GS, which was the factory's designation for the four-cam model in Grand

American client. The car took almost three years to complete and is reputed to have cost more than $250,000 to build.

At first glance this would not appear to be the definitive 911 factory-built custom, and in many respects it is not up to the purely visual tenets established by the 930 *Flachtbau* cars assembled at the Works. It is, however, the most extensive custom-built 911 ever produced and an extraordinary example of just how far Special Works is willing to go to satisfy a customer's requests.

Special edition Porsches all began with a single idea, the America Roadster, built to order for Porsche's U.S. importer, Max Hoffman, in 1952. Hoffman purchased 15 of the 16 cars produced, putting them into the hands of noted American race drivers Briggs Cunningham, Richie Ginther, Phil Walters, John Bentley, Jack McAfee, and John and Josie von Neumann. The lightweight, aluminum-bodied racer became the legitimate forerunner of the famed 356 Speedster.

Contrasting the exterior color scheme, the luxurious leather upholstery was a special dye lot in Doric Gray, accented with burgundy seat piping—one of the few instances where Porsche seats have had contrasting trim.

In 1980 a limited-edition model, to honor the men of Weissach, Porsche's engineering department, was introduced. The special 911SC Weissach Coupe was limited to only 400 examples, half painted a distinctive Metallic Black, the others Platinum Metallic, both colors exclusive to the Weissach models. The model was also equipped with the Turbo tail, the only normally aspirated 911 model to come from the factory with this feature in 1980.

Sport trim. The consummate example of what the Special Works Department is capable of, the America GS was fitted with a one-of-a-kind interior, upholstered throughout with hand-dyed leather, a specially mixed one-off exterior color, and distinctive exterior bodywork.

In general, a customer requests a Special Works Department car through a local dealer, but that request is usually limited to paint color or interior color and special leather and wood trim options, such as the yellow Carrera 4 Cabriolet pictured in this chapter from the Kent Rawson collection. Both Rawson's C4 and the America GS could be likened to purchasing a tailored suit versus one off the rack. Both of these extraordinary

examples are best described in old world taxonomy as "bespoke": one made from scratch.

The story of the America GS begins in 1989. On the occasion of Dr. Ferry Porsche's 80th birthday, the company built a one-off model called the Panamericana, which was designed by Lagaay. He was contacted by an American who had previously had a Special Works 930 built and now wanted to know if he could have a car along the same lines as the Panamericana. After several conversations, Lagaay sent off some concept sketches for a custom-built wide-body Cabriolet. At the time, in 1990, there were no set plans at Porsche AG to produce a wide-body Carrera 2 Cabriolet or the America Roadster, yet this was very close to what Lagaay

The America GS color scheme is blue-green with purple accents, which looks much better than it sounds. The leather used throughout the car was specially selected and then hand-dyed by Roser, which supplies Porsche with its upholstery. A three-stage dye process—actually more like silkscreening—was required, starting with a base coat of gray followed by a layer of purple and then a layer of green, creating a marbleized effect. Every item from the bezels surrounding the instruments to door handles, vents, the day/night rearview mirror toggle, down to the control knobs, is hand finished in either green or purple leather.

The interior features a hand-made center console to house a specially manufactured 11-band graphic equalizer, AM/FM cassette/CD stereo system, six individual compact disc trays, and operating switches for the rear spoiler, telephone, and central locking and warning systems. The America GS is equipped with a race-tuned Tiptronic and competition RS engine.

sketched out. It was by chance that the design of the Special Works car coincided with the introduction of the commemorative 911 models, and in a backhanded way, one could consider this the original design for the 1992 America Roadster!

The America GS shares a similar color scheme with Dr. Porsche's Panamericana, using a mixture of Metallic Green and purple for both the exterior paint (which takes on an almost aqua tint in daylight) and the leather interior. When Lagaay designed the America GS, he prepared a series of color pallets showing exterior and interior combinations, accent trim, upholstery, and carpeting. In all, there were eight different versions, with the green and purple blend finally being selected. At that point, the owner flew to Zuffenhausen to meet with Lagaay and Special Works director Rolf Sprenger. This was almost unprecedented and would ultimately involve many of Porsche's outside suppliers needed to manufacture special components for the car, either in Metallic Green or purple.

The mere complexities of a simple color change from OEM became almost mind boggling. Even a rudimentary item like the zipper for the rear window in the Cabriolet top presented an interesting challenge: To have it match the purple leather trim a minimum run of 400 zippers had to be ordered, just to get one! Now, what does one do with 399 extra purple zippers?

For the America GS, Metallic Green wheels and purple brake calipers involved the services of both BBS in Germany and Brembo in Italy. The outside suppliers all had to agree on the specific shades of green and purple. Explains the owner, who traveled to Italy to discuss manufacturing four purple brake calipers with Brembo management, "You are dealing with companies that are not equipped to build special items these days, so it takes a great deal of time and personal effort to get this kind of work done." Procuring the BBS wheels was a similar experience. Historically, BBS has supplied wheels to Porsche for race cars, but not for production models. Having BBS manufacture a set of 8x17 and 9.5x17 rims for the America GS was yet another special order. To get the exact finish the owner wanted, BBS had to paint the wheels before assembly, opposite the usual

procedure, thus requiring a great deal of extra attention and hand labor during assembly to prevent damage to the paint. You end up with a very expensive set of wheels.

At the Special Works Department a never-before-attempted removable hardtop, equipped with a power sunroof, interior lights, and a rear window defroster, was being fabricated. A project that would take months to complete with the intricate wiring harnesses and relays needed to link the removable top to the 911's electrical system.

The Works also fitted the America with a Carrera Cup Motronic Engine Management System and upgraded the engine to produce in excess of 280 horsepower and 260 lb-ft of torque. (This was later redone with a race-tuned Tiptronic and competition RS engine.) To handle the additional power, various suspension designs were evaluated to find one that would

The one-off America GS was designed by Porsche's chief stylist Harm Lagaay. The Special Works car started out as one of the 40th anniversary 911 widebody Cabriolets. The "GS" epithet comes from the old 356 Carrera GS, which was the factory's designation for the four-cam model in Grand Sport trim. The America GS wears a specially mixed exterior color created by Lagaay. This is the only Porsche ever produced in this color.

The 911 America Roadster, debuted in 1992 as a limited-edition model commemorating the 40th anniversary of the original 356 models. This example, based on the Carrera 2 widebody Cabriolet, was a specially commissioned version produced by Porsche's Special Works Department. It actually predated the design of limited-edition 911 America Roadsters. This was in essence the prototype, although not officially.

At various times Porsche introduces special limited-edition models intended for club sport racing, such as the 1993–1994 RS America, a modern-day version of the original Carrera RS 2.7 first seen in 1973. The RS Americas were powered by the normally aspirated Carrera 3.6-liter engine. The lightweight RS America became the quickest accelerating nonturbo model, capable of 0 to 60 in 5.4 seconds and a top speed of 162 miles per hour.

bring the America GS closest to competition specifications, without putting undue stress on the body.

The car itself, basically a stock Carrera 2 wide-body Cabriolet, had a Group B spoiler added to the rear wing, and in front, the bumper was modified to accept combination projector fog lights and functional front oil cooler/air conditioning condenser cooling ducts, in place of the standard fog lights. These are features you simply do not order through your local Porsche dealer.

The interior was treated to similar special attention with a handmade, custom upholstered center console, added to house a specially manufactured 11-band graphic equalizer, the AM/FM cassette/compact disc stereo system, six individual compact disc trays, and operating switches for the rear spoiler, telephone, central locking, and warning systems. As a result of the center console design, the Porsche cellular phone—built by Fujitsu and offered as an option on 911 models—had to be repositioned farther back on the center tunnel, in turn requiring a custom-built hands-free speaker that was ingeniously hidden beneath the parking brake lever! *Labor*. Lots of labor.

The custom electronics system for the America incorporates an innovative Hirschmann antenna that combines cellular phone reception with AM/FM. Operating independently of the radio when a call is received, it eliminates the need for an unsightly cellular antenna on the windshield or third brake light housing.

The leather used throughout the car was specially selected and then hand-dyed by Roser, which supplies Porsche with its upholstery. Lagaay's color scheme required a three-stage dye process—actually more like silk screening—that began with a base coat of gray, followed by a layer of purple, and then a layer

of green, creating a marblized effect. The carpet was also dyed to match the leather, and it took the manufacturer four attempts to reproduce Lagaay's color specifications.

Other interior design hurdles included the RS Carrera Cup race seats, which were upholstered in full leather. This is generally not done by Recaro because of the shape of the Carrera Cup seatbacks. The leather had to be bonded to the framework with a special 3M adhesive. The material for the seatbelts, like the previously mentioned purple zipper, also had to be custom made, and you don't manufacture just enough to do one pair of belts—it comes in great rolls 100 yards long. Cut off just enough for the GS, and you have a lifetime supply of purple webbing left over. And then there is handwork—leather surfaces cover the entire interior, and every item from the bezels surrounding the instruments, to door handles, vents, the day/night rearview mirror toggle, down to the control knobs— every piece is hand finished in either green or purple leather. Obsessive? Perhaps, but precision craftsmanship at this level becomes obsessive. Special Works team members even went beyond the parameters set down by Lagaay, making leather caps to cover screwheads, and even a leather-covered emergency brake handle with embossed P O R S C H E lettering. The design study notebook for the America GS had more than 215 separate entries requiring individual custom work!

Kent Rawson's 1994 C4 Cabriolet is a prime example of what the Special Works Department normally delivers. Custom colors are one of the Work's specialties. The colors for Rawson's C4 are Champagne Yellow, with Afrika Korps beige fabric for the Cabriolet top. The interior, dashboard, and door caps were

Porsche's *Jubiläumsmodell* 911 Carrera 4 was produced in a special series to commemorate the 911's 30th year. The cars were distinctively badged with the 911 insignia and *30 Jahre* on the rear decklid. *Porsche AG*

done in cashmere leather rather than the traditional black. The dashboard trim, steering wheel, and shifter were hand-finished rootwood, and the seats were made to order with plaid inserts. The center console was also custom fabricated and similar to the design created for the America GS. And, like the America, all of the interior trim was covered in leather, including the instrument bezels, air vents, and all of the control knobs.

The engine on the C4 was left stock, except for a sport exhaust system. Far less complicated than the America GS, the C4 Cabriolet still took eight months to complete.

Occasionally, interior trim features developed for customers in Special Works find their way into other limited production models, such as the 1997 Turbo S, which has a number of special features developed at the Works. The appeal of a car like the America GS, however, is undoubtedly limited, as are the number of enthusiasts with the money to have such a car built. There was a time when exclusive automobiles were all handmade, however. Bodies were hammered out of flat stock, interiors were carved from fine wood, upholstery was handsewn, and fabrics and colors were personally selected. For most

of the world that time has passed, and those venerable skills have become little more than anachronisms. Fortunately, for those who desire the finer things that roll on four wheels, there are places like the Special Works Department at Porsche AG.

While Porsche has never been prone to overstatement, Zuffenhausen has, on occasion, produced some strictly limited editions to commemorate the anniversaries of earlier models, production milestones, or to meet the needs of sports car club competition. To celebrate the 30th anniversary of the 911, for example, Porsche produced a limited-edition Carrera 4 Coupe with Turbo fender flares and 17-inch wheels. The edition of, appropriately, 911 cars, was produced in a special violet-metallic color with Rubicon Gray interior upholstery and subtle detail accents such as a silver-colored metal plate on the rear package shelf bearing the sequential number of the car in the 30 *Jahre* commemorative series. A semimatte silver emblem below the 911 insignia on the rear deck lid also read 30 *Jahre*.

Another special edition 911 was also produced to mark the firm's 25th anniversary back in 1975. These featured a plaque on the glovebox door with Ferry Porsche's signature and the number

Another Porsche that was exclusive to the European market was the road version of the 911 GT 2 built in 1995. This was essentially a street legal race car. *Porsche AG*

of the car within the series of 400 produced. The cars were painted Silver Metallic and made available in both Coupe and Targa versions. The seats were a distinctive blue-black leatherette with "Tweed" fabric inserts. The door panels, rear side panels, rear panel, rear seat cushions, and rear backrests were in blue-black tweed.

Other significant benchmarks were noted with special models such as the 1988 series produced in Blue Diamond Metallic to celebrate the sale of the 250,000th 911. The cars were set off by color-matched Fuchs wheels, silver-gray carpeting, and

silver-blue leather upholstery with Ferry Porsche's signature stitched into the headrests. A total of 875 were produced, in Coupe, Cabriolet, and Targa versions.

In 1980 Porsche produced a limited-edition 911SC model known as the Weissach Coupe. This was a particularly difficult time for sports car manufacturers. Gasoline shortages and increasing federal regulations were making "performance" a word that was best whispered, and here in the throes of expanding global conservatism was Porsche, along with a handful of other European marques, manufacturing thoroughbred sports cars for a world that had suddenly shifted its automotive priorities from miles per hour to miles per gallon.

While automakers the world over were scrambling to build economy-minded cars, Zuffenhausen relinquished little, save for a willful gesture, limiting speedometers to read a maximum of 85 miles per hour on cars shipped to the United States. The cars, or course, could do almost twice that. Compromise was never a consideration; Americans learned to read the tachometer.

Its image intact, both on the road and in motorsports competition, Porsche unveiled the 172-brake horsepower 911SC Weissach Coupe, to be produced in a limited series of 400 cars, half painted a distinctive Metallic Black, the others Platinum Metallic. The colors would be exclusive to the Weissach Coupes in 1980 and both versions were luxuriously upholstered in Doric Gray, accented with burgundy seat piping and rust-colored carpeting.

The cars were equipped with the 930-style Turbo Tail, a popular after-purchase modification made on hundreds of 911SC models, but the Weissach Coupes were the only factory-built cars to come so equipped. Sales literature for the 911SC model proclaimed it ". . . one of the most exclusive production cars you can own. The Limited Edition Weissach Coupe has been produced to honor the men of Weissach, who have made this series what it is." The Weissach Coupes were designed with a competitive edge and equipped with a sport suspension and Pirelli CN36 tires—185/70 VR15 front, 215/60 VR15 rear. All 400 cars were sold in the United States.

Always competition minded, Porsche occasionally comes up with a limited-edition 911 model intended for sports car club racing. One of the rarest was the Club Sport, which was produced twice, once in 1987 as a lightweight (stripped) base 911 sold in Great Britain, Germany, and the United States, and again in 1996 as the 911 Carrera RS Clubsport, equipped with a 3,746-cc, 300-brake horsepower engine, special front spoiler, flared rear fenders, and rear spoiler. The factory also produced a road version of the 911 GT 2 in 1995. Neither the Clubsport nor GT 2 was sold in the United States.

In 1993 and 1994, there was the 911 RS America, introduced as a club racer and the lowest-priced 911 model of the year at $54,800, more than $10,000 lower than the Carrera 2. Porsche was once again commemorating its past, only this time with a car that *could* be sold in the United States.

The RS America traced its roots back to the Carrera RS 2.7 of 1973, which by the early 1990s, had become one of the most sought after Porsche models of all time.

In its introduction of the RS America, Porsche noted that, "The original Porsche 911 Carrera RS led to the RSR, a special racing model which won the 24 Hours of Daytona and the 12 Hours of Sebring in 1973. In the process, the RSR earned Porsche the IMSA Drivers Championship as well as the Manu-

Porsche honored the Carrera RS in 1996 with a special lightweight model known as the RS Clubsport. Built for sports car club competition, the limited-edition 911 Carrera was not offered for sale in the United States.

facturers Championship. The RS formed the starting point of Porsche's decade-long domination of production-based GT racing with the RSR, 934, and 935."

It was with this historical imperative that Porsche designed the RS America to emulate the first 911 Carrera models. The cars were equipped with corduroy Recaro bucket seats, and the rear fold-down seats were replaced with a flat parcel shelf with two lockable storage bins (thus becoming a legitimate two-place model like the 911 Speedster). Most of the sound insulation from the RS America was eliminated, the door panels had no armrests or storage panels, and the door latch was released by a nylon pull strap. Basically it was a modern version of the Carrera RS 2.7 lightweight.

The cars were powered by the normally aspirated 3.6-liter engine, which combined with the RS America's lighter weight, was able to reach higher levels of performance than the Carrera 2. It was the quickest accelerating nonturbo model, capable of 0 to 60 in 5.4 seconds and a top test track speed of 162 miles per hour. Intended for club racing, the America was not available with air conditioning. The RS came standard with larger, wider 17-inch wheels and tires, more aggressive spring and shock absorber tuning, a larger front stabilizer bar, and steering was nonassisted rack and pinion. It was a club racer in the fullest sense.

As Porsche celebrates its 50th anniversary in 1998, the 911 is poised to begin a new era, and with it will no doubt come other limited-edition models, as well as custom-built examples from Rolf Sprenger's Special Works Department. Cars for the 21st century that will carry on a tradition that appears to have no end in sight.

CHAPTER SEVEN

CARRERA 4

A 959 for the Road

Porsche's first major production efforts toward an all-wheel-drive model were the Type 959, which introduced all-new technology. The AWD system pioneered on the 959 led the way to the Carrera 4, introduced in 1989. The 959 has probably become the most sensationalized model in Porsche history because of its limited production, unavailability as a street legal model for the United States, and racing history in the FIA's Group B category. The 1986 Paris-Dakar Turbo 959s made the cars legendary, finishing first, second, and sixth in the 22-day marathon. The road-going versions became the most sought-after and expensive 911 derivatives ever built. *Randy Leffingwell*

The 959 interior design was almost identical to that of a 911, although a quick look around the cockpit hints at a different agenda. There is a subtle all-wheel-drive indicator at the top of the oil and water temperature gauge, a 340-kilometer-per-hour speedometer, (actual top speed 315 kilometers per hour or 196 miles per hour), and shift console-mounted controls for adjusting ride height and shock absorber damping. The 959 also had a six-speed gearbox. *Randy Leffingwell*

Speed. You can feel it. Breathe it. And you can question it. How fast can the car go? What limits can it reach? How fast can I go? What are my limits?

In many production automobiles, that limit is usually attained around 120 miles per hour. And at that, for most cars (and most drivers), traveling at 2 miles per minute is testing the very mettle of their abilities. For a select few automobiles, that boundary has extended into the rarefied reaches of 150 miles per hour; and, for an even more exclusive handful, velocities teetering on the edge of 200 miles per hour.

At this moment in time, however, on this road in the south of France, the speedometer needle is playing with the 160-mile-per-hour line. The engine is turning at maximum revs. The exhaust note is as melodious in the cold morning air as the call of Ulysses' sirens, matched only in tone and intensity by the howl of air rushing over the car's rooftop and deflecting off the side mirrors. At this clip, the world passes by in a torrent of wind and color. Yet, at two and a half times the limit we're allowed to drive on American highways (Montana notwithstanding . . .), there is an uncanny sense of security behind the familiar wheel of the Porsche Carrera 4.

The 959 engine was a veritable testbed for Weissach engineers. The twin-turbocharged boxer design used water-cooled four-valve cylinder heads mounted on air-cooled cylinders—a hybrid mixed cooling system adapted from the 956/962 racing engine. The turbos were activated progressively, a technology Porsche dubbed *Registeraufladung* or sequential turbocharging, which employed a small initial turbocharger for loads under 4,300 rpm, after which a second, larger turbo (already being spooled up) kicked in for high-load, high-rpm duty. The 959 developed a remarkable 450 brake horsepower from only 2.85 liters. *Randy Leffingwell*

All-wheel drive was anything but new to Porsche. A four-wheel-drive Volkswagen developed in the 1930s was produced during World War II in a variety of forms. In the early 1980s, Porsche produced 4x4 911s for competition, such as this model built for the 1983 Paris-Dakar race. Known as the Type 953, the car was powered by a 3.2-liter engine. *Porsche AG*

It is here that the old and the new have come together in what appears to be perfect harmony—a synergy between man and machine that must be maintained to preserve the 911's traditional values, which are critically important to the purist loyalists of the Zuffenhausen breed. Since its introduction in 1989 this has been the Porsche 911 personified. This devotion to the "only true" Porsches—those with their air-cooled engines tucked neatly in the rear—is rewarded by the Carrera 4, a car that represents over a quarter-century of development, but is still, curiously, as much the same as it is different from the first 911 models.

Professor Helmuth Bott, who spearheaded the 959 program at Porsche in 1983, noted that with the new technology they were developing for the 959, the objective was ". . . to show the people, without changing the concept, this car, the 911, is capable of completely different things. . . ." Tony Lapine, who had begun his career as a General Motors stylist in 1952, was the head of Porsche's design studio during the 959's development, and he too recognized the importance of the car and its potential impact on future Porsche models. There was a design legacy. "From Komenda, from Butzi? Certainly. Definitely. Absolutely. I understood my job as being the custodian of the tradition. I may improve on it, but I may not change it. Changing is easy," said Lapine. "Improving on it is harder, much harder." This was the foundation for the 911's evolution. The substance of the 959 and its influence on the Carrera 4's development afterward.

However similar to previous 911s, the Carrera 4 appears on the outside—traditional windshield, doors, roofline, fenders, and trunk lid—beneath that familiar veneer lives a fully independent coil-spring suspension, antilock brake system, power-assisted rack-and-pinion steering, and four-wheel-drive system generations ahead of anything Porsche engineers could have imagined in 1964. As much as it may visually resemble all 911s, 85 percent of the Carrera 4's components have no ties to the past!

There is more than a hint of what lies beneath the Carrera 4's comely exterior, if one considers the design characteristics gleaned from Porsche's quarter-million-dollar all-wheel-drive 959 (and subsequent 961) competition cars. At both ends the bumpers have a similar appearance, the front with the 959's functional air intakes. At the rear, the overstated whale tail has been replaced by a subtle, integrally mounted wing, which rises out of the engine cover to apply the necessary downforce at speeds above 48 miles per hour. Underneath, the Carrera 4 is virtually sealed by a full-length belly pan, which reduces both the amount of noise emanating from the car and the admission of road noise into the passenger compartment.

At its worst, the Carrera 4 is the best Porsche ever. At its best, it is one of the most thoroughly competent road-going sports cars in the world—comfortable, easy to drive, and practical enough to undertake even mundane motoring tasks. From behind the wheel there are many changes, yet it still seems as though there have been few. The all-new chassis and all-wheel-drive system introduced in 1989 repositioned the gearbox so that it falls more readily at hand, and yet even the most modern Porsche interior is no more than a luxurious redress of the original.

Light the 3.6-liter engine, and there is that same air-cooled, six-cylinder rumble from behind. Tease the throttle, and the whine is music to a Porsche owner's ears.

Play it.

Push the pedal and the Carrera 4 consumes 0 to 60 in five and a half seconds. At the upper reaches of 150 miles per hour, the driver can sense that the four driven wheels are firmly in touch with the road, that the power-assist steering is ever so precise, and that the antilock disc brakes can scrub off speed with unfaltering reliability in an instant. Confidence. That is what the driver feels most behind the wheel of a C4.

At the heart of the Carrera 4 is an all-wheel-drive system that, surprisingly, was not derived from the 959, but uses an entirely new and less costly design. It divides torque through a mechanical center differential, delivering 31 percent of the drive force to the front wheels and 69 percent to the rear, under normal driving conditions. When needed, the system automatically directs more power to the wheels offering the best traction. In practice, you can't tell when it's working, except for the indicator light on the dash.

With one car, Porsche again redefined the 911. It was the Carrera 4, the production evolution of the legendary 959 Group B car. Although the Carrera 4 was similar in appearance to previous 911 models, 85 percent of its components had no ties to the earlier 911 designs. Beneath the familiar veneer of windshield, doors, roofline, fenders, and trunk lid was a revised independent coil-spring suspension design, antilock brakes, power-assisted rack-and-pinion steering, and an all-wheel-drive system generations ahead of anything Porsche had to offer a year before the Carrera 4's introduction.

The famous Porsche whale-tail was replaced on the Carrera 4 with a newly designed retractable wing integrally mounted to the deck lid. The wing can be manually raised or lowered from a dash-mounted switch or will automatically extend at speeds above 48 miles per hour and retract when the car comes to a stop. This has since become a standard feature on all Porsche models except Turbos.

Porsche hasn't exactly rewritten the laws of physics with its all-wheel-drive system, but let's say they've tampered with a few of its precepts. Our first opportunity to drive the Carrera 4 was back in 1989, in the south of France, where we were allowed to open it up and experience first-hand what this car had to offer. Cruising along tree-lined country roads on the outskirts of Saint-Paul de Vence, we pressed the car into corners at speeds that would have exposed us to the dreaded and perilous 911 oversteer, requiring deft counter-steer, often followed by a solemn oath never to do that again! Knowing this, it was at first confounding to drive a 911 with neutral handling, that when pushed harder into a turn develops a slight tendency toward understeer. Though contrary to past experience, it was nonetheless so. The Carrera 4 does not feel like a 911 in the classic sense, but so much the better.

Zuffenhausen geared up for the 911 Carrera 4 in a big way. Here cars are seen awaiting shipment in 1989. The C4 was one of the most successful new model launches in Porsche history. *Porsche AG*

With this improved level of responsiveness comes an element of what we'll call Carrera euphoria, which beckons you to press the car deeper into turns. To our surprise and relief, if you err (as we did) and lift in a curve (a normal, often regrettable reaction when you realize there isn't enough road), everything works as Porsche's engineers had promised. The dynamically controlled all-wheel-drive system instantly redistributes torque to keep the car in shape. The Carrera 4 held the line, and we swore that terrible oath.

One improvement that almost goes unnoticed is Porsche's power-assisted steering, which manages to enhance the car's handling without taking away any of that wonderful feedback that 911s have always provided. What has been erased from the steering is the tendency for the wheel to be wrenched from your hands when encountering a bump in the middle of a turn. You no longer have to manhandle the car in corners. The power assist handles the counterforce; you handle the car. Another 911 tradition shed, but one that will not be missed.

While the changes that set the Carrera 4 apart from its 911 heritage are subtle at best, Porsche's most advanced design

improvements go unseen; unless, of course, you slide underneath the car and look up. What you'll see is . . . nothing. Just like the bottom side of a 959.

The most important part of aerodynamics is minimizing resistance to the flow of air over the body of the car. But, equally important, though seldom addressed, is the resistance to airflow from beneath. Thus, the Carrera 4 became the first production Porsche to offer a full-length belly pan, the underside almost totally enclosed by plastic and metal panels. The engine itself is encapsulated by a full pan, bordered on either side by molded plastic panels. Also fully enclosed is the exhaust system. Except for the wheels and outer perimeter of the suspension, everything is concealed. While reducing exposed area, the panels also retain heat, so the functional air intakes in the front of the bumper are used to direct air through the sealed undercarriage to assist in cooling the transmission, engine, and antilock brake system.

In their overall application, the undercarriage panels serve several purposes. Foremost are the obvious aerodynamic gains provided by a smooth unobstructed surface—in theory, a race car-proven ground effects design; moreover, the enclosure was designed to reduce the level of noise emanating from the engine compartment in compliance with European regulations, making the Carrera 4 noticeably quieter than previous 911s. In turn, this also reduces exterior road noise entering the passenger compartment, providing an uncommonly quiet interior environment. Not too quiet, of course. You still get a proper mixture of engine, transmission, and exhaust sound, but fewer bumps and tharumps invade from the pavement below.

With the Carrera 4, Porsche managed to establish a new generation of cars with enhanced aerodynamics, handling, and performance, while at the same time avoiding an attack on holy

Porsche addressed many of the old line complaints about Spartan luxury in the 911 with the introduction of the C4, adding the stylish center console and more luxurious upholstery and trim.

Photographed at the introduction in France, the Carrera 4 coupe was the beginning of a new dynasty of 911 models that would re-establish the marque and sustain the 911 well into the 1990s.

911 standards. A compromise? Perhaps. But how else can the old and the new exist together in harmony?

Back in 1989, Carrera 4 technology was only available on the 911 Coupe. Since then, the all-wheel-drive system has been extended throughout the Porsche line, and in 1996, the Turbo was added, creating the most powerful and best-handling 911 in the company's history, followed in 1997 by the very limited Turbo S model, offering special "S" features and a 424-brake horsepower twin-turbocharged, twin-intercooled engine.

The enhanced 3.6-liter boxer delivers a chest-swelling load of power to the car's 18-inch "Technology" polished-look wheels, and does so in what seems like milliseconds.

The 993 series brought about a sweeping evolution of the 911 shape, with sensuously flowing fenderlines and integrated headlights, taillights, and bumpers. The 1996 Turbo, pictured, was the ultimate extension of the 911 design, equipped with second-generation Carrera 4 all-wheel-drive technology and a 400-brake horsepower twin-turbocharged and intercooled engine.

In this car you can forget about breathtaking acceleration—with the Turbo S it's gasping acceleration, in every gear and at every speed. First to second sets you back in the seat after a moment's lag and second to third at full song—with the bellow of the engine filling the cockpit—is a perfect accompaniment to the ever-increasing g force. For the first several seconds it's almost Wagnerian grandeur—trumpets blaring *Flight of the Valkyries*, as an aggressive 400-foot-pound torque, dispensed through the six-speed gearbox, reels in the distance with alarming haste. So

much power is unleashed from the twin-turbocharged 3.6 that the car dashes from 0 to 60 in just a click over 4 seconds, and with little more than a delayed shift to third at full throttle 100 miles per hour is a mere five beats away. This car gets fast, so fast that you need to watch even the most innocent indulgence of speed or you're into triple digits. Needless to say, the Turbo S is not for the timid, or the underinsured.

The greatest problem with past 911 Turbos has been the ability of drivers to manage power and handling. The original

The widebody look has become synonymous with high-performance Porsche models. Pictured are the last of the air-cooled breed, the Carrera 4S and 911 Turbo all-wheel-drive models.

Turbo model of 1975 proved to be more than a handful for most owners, and the number of damaged cars within the first year validated Porsche's suspicion that giving customers what they wanted—a street version of a factory race car—wasn't necessarily a good idea. Subsequent Turbo 911s have softened the edge, but what it really took to make this car viable for the road was the C4's all-wheel drive. As sure-footed as the Carrera 4, the Turbo S has a decided advantage in brute power. What the C4 Turbo serves up as standard fare would have been considered a factory race car just a few years ago! The Turbo S uses the same AWD system from the 993 Carrera 4. At only 111 pounds, this system is half the weight of the earlier 964 C4 and 33 percent more efficient in operation, with the viscous center-clutch controlling power distribution to all four wheels as needed to maintain ideal traction. The system gives the Turbo S perfectly neutral handling and turn in that feels as though the car is mounted on rails. All of the ills of the past are gone. What you find is a car with turbo power and Carrera 4 handling, a marriage made of technology that all but defies the laws of road physics.

For $150,000, this car so far exceeds our expectations as to rival the Lamborghini Diablo VT, priced at $100,000 more, and to vanquish all Ferraris short of the $500,000 F50. Too much praise? Call it infatuation with perfection. Porsche has ended the air-cooled 911's career on a high note by taking the design as far as it could possibly go. Seems we've heard that line before. Back in 1976 the 245-brake horsepower Turbo Carrera was

PORSCHE GT1

By Stephen R. Ruddock

The surprising win by a BMW-powered McLaren F1 GTR at Le Mans in 1995 sent the management of Porsche into a grueling reassessment of its objectives. As a result, for the first time in two decades Porsche would add a totally new car to its model line-up in 1996. Taking the checkered flag had always resulted in greater showroom traffic and sales for Porsche, and with the 911's history in motorsports at stake, Porsche needed a high-profile victory at the world's most famous sports car race to preserve that tradition.

In 1995 Porsche had spent a great deal of money to build and develop a car to compete in IMSA's World Sports Car category. The TWR Porsche was designed to compete at Daytona, Sebring, and Le Mans, with the intent of bolstering the sales of Porsche road cars. However, when the TWR Porsches showed up for prerace testing at Daytona, their speed caused the sanctioning body to change the rules at the last minute. The rules makers wanted Porsche to add weight to the cars and decrease the diameter of the engine intake restriction. Such changes conjured memories of Porsche's Indianapolis debacle in 1980, and the company canceled the project and put the cars into storage.

For 1996 the FIA Working Group approved regulations that would allow a manufacturer to homologate a new race car and only build one road-legal example that would be for sale at the same time. The idea was to encourage manufacturers to produce production-based GT cars that would be less costly to build and campaign than out-and-out prototypes. Unfortunately, the FIA's concept was flawed. In reality, when designing a new race car, it is more efficient to start with a clean sheet of paper than to work with existing parts. The FIA ruling left Porsche to make a difficult decision, but with just eight months to prepare for the 1996 Le Mans race, Porsche management gave the green light to the project. The GT1 program was assigned to Porsche's guru of go, Norbert Singer.

Before a car can be certified for road use in Europe it must first be crash tested. With time running out, Porsche decided to use the steel front structure of the 993 as a starting point for the new car. This allowed the engineers to save precious time by skipping the crash testing because data was already on file.

In order to be competitive in the GT class, it was decided to place the engine in front of the rear wheels, thereby allowing considerable advantages in handling and chassis setup over previous GT cars. Singer was also charged with the task of incorporating styling elements which would make the GT1 resemble its brethren, even though beneath the skin it would be pure race car. Due to the time crunch, however, Porsche

FLAMES lick the track as the Porsche GT1 streaks down the straight at Colorado's Pikes Peak International Raceway. The car's sleek body styling is a perfect translation of the 911. *Stephen R. Ruddock*

PORSCHE GT1 making good time at Laguna Seca Raceway in October 1997. *Stephen R. Ruddock*

decided to use its fully water-cooled flat-six engine in the GT1. With proven reliability and some 600 horsepower on tap, use of this engine simplified Singer's job, allowing more time for suspension and aerodynamic development.

By using many off-the-shelf components in the GT1's construction, the Weissach *werke* was able to fire up and start testing the first car only 234 days after the original drawings for the car were completed. A program of testing and development at Weissach's private test track was begun immediately, as well as extended tests at the famed Paul Ricard circuit. The Porsche team was able to pile up 11,000 kilometers at speed before shipping two cars to the Sarthe for the world's most prestigious endurance race.

The GT1s finished first and second in class, second and third overall, with the win, ironically, going to the TWR Porsche, which had been taken out of storage and leased to the Joest team, which had won in 1984 and 1985.

The Le Mans victory was a huge marketing success for Porsche, which again proved to the world that its ability to build champion sports cars, even in a relatively short time, is unequalled by any other manufacturer, big or small.

The 600-horsepower, fully water-cooled flat-six engine in the GT1 is positioned in front of the rear wheels, thereby allowing considerable advantages in handling and chassis setup over previous GT cars. *Stephen R. Ruddock*

In the pits at Laguna Seca, October 26, 1997. *Stephen R. Ruddock*

The last of the air-cooled 911 Turbos, the 1997 Turbo S was equipped with a stylish whale tail treatment unique to the Turbo body.

described by automotive magazines as "the ultimate extension of the 911."

They were, perhaps, a bit premature in that opinion.

With the Turbo S, Porsche delivered the best car in 911 history with uncompromised power, unerring stability on the road, ABS 5 antilock brakes, improved suspension, and the venerable boxer engine assisted by dual intercoolers and twin turbos.

For anyone who may have forgotten, this is the car Porsche enthusiasts have been waiting for since 1985, when the legendary 959 made its debut. Acknowledged as one of the greatest cars of the 20th century, the 959 was a limited-edition model designed for competition and European roads and was never allowed into the United States except for racing or display in a museum. That isn't to say a few road miles weren't accumulated by a handful of 959s that crossed the Atlantic in the late 1980s, but the 959 was never legally allowed on American roads.

The 1997 Porsche 911 Turbo features the same engine and drivetrain concept as the 959 but in a less expensive, and in the opinion of some, better looking, production version designed to be driven daily on North American roads.

To be fair, the 911 Turbo, aside from speed and agility, is no different than any other 911 model, with the exception of the larger Turbo Tail. The interior is the same traditional Porsche design, nicely tailored in leather, but no more or less distinctive. That may be its only drawback. No one notices this car unless you blow past them at 100 miles per hour, which in most states is still unpopular with the local constabulary. Then again, being unobtrusive is more in vogue these days, and the Carrera 4 Turbo delivers on its promise of unmatched performance in such a way that most casual observers will never know what passed them.

THE 1997 Turbo S sported the most luxurious interior ever offered on a 911. The limited-edition model featured special interior colors including "brick," which aptly describes the earthen hue of this Turbo S upholstery.

There's an engine in there somewhere under the air-to-air intercooler housing, which draws through the vents in front of the Turbo tail.

The last word in Turbo models was the "S," introduced as a limited-edition model in 1997 with special interior and exterior styling, a 425-brake horsepower engine, and a staggering $150,000 price tag.

CHAPTER EIGHT

1998 AND BEYOND

The Last Air-Cooled 911 Models

With the Turbo bowing out for the 1998 model year, the Carrera 4S, combining the widebody Turbo look with the Porsche all-wheel-drive powertrain, becomes Zuffenhausen's top coupe. Included with the Carrera 4S are Turbo-look 18-inch pressure-cast alloy wheels and the same power-assisted, internally vented four-piston disc brakes used on the 911 Turbo. The Carrera 4S six-speed manual gearbox is optimized for smooth, light, and precise shifting. The side rocker panels and wider rear fenders of the Carrera 4S were adapted from the 1997 Porsche 911 Turbo. Rather than the Turbo tail, the Carrera 4S has a speed-dependent, extendable rear spoiler identical to other 911 models.

The 1997–1998 Porsche Boxster sets the pace for the next generation 911. The new age Speedster is the first water-cooled mid-engine production car in Porsche's history. The benchmark design also provides the platform for the 1999 Carrera models, which replaced the last air-cooled 993 Porsches at the end of model year 1998. *Porsche AG*

The 1998 model year marks the end of a 35-year era in Porsche history—these will be the last 911 models powered by an air-cooled flat-six boxer engine, with the exception of the 911 Targa, which will be carried over into the 1999 model year. In that respect alone, the 1998 coupes and cabriolets may become the most collectable 911s of this decade. The last of anything is always afforded special prominence among enthusiasts.

The air-cooled 911 ends its career almost as it started, in coupe, targa, and cabriolet versions, albeit in a far more contemporary idiom with available all-wheel-drive for coupe and cabriolet models.

Porsche's on-again, off-again affair with the turbo is off once more as the twin turbocharged and intercooled Carrera all-wheel-drive Turbo and Turbo S (1996, 1997) bow out from Zuffenhausen's elite 1998 line-up of Carrera models. In preparation for the all-new 996 series, the Turbos have been chosen as the first models to be phased out.

Porsche celebrates its golden anniversary in 1998 with the best built and most technologically advanced cars in its history and an international reputation that's been built upon the framework of the original 911, an automobile that has not only withstood the test of time, but through its unparalleled longevity established standards that no other auto maker has ever approached. Five distinct body styles are in the 1998 Porsche 911 stable: the Carrera S Coupe "widebody" with Turbo-style fender treatment; the Carrera Cabriolet, which uses the standard 911 body shell; the Carrera 4S Coupe, which combines the widebody look with the Porsche all-wheel-drive powertrain; the Carrera 4 Cabriolet, incorporating all-wheel drive and a convertible body style; and the glass-top Carrera Targa, introduced in 1996.

The Carrera S Coupe, which made its debut in March 1997 at the New York International Auto Show, incorporates the wide front and rear bodywork of the 911 Turbo and 911 Carrera 4S, with a split rear spoiler grille, "Cup Design" 17-inch alloy wheels, steel gray interior trim, black leather instrument panel and door trim, and Carrera S identification on the rear engine cover. This becomes the entry-level 911, with all of these features at no price increase compared to the 1997 Carrera Coupe.

For the air-cooled boxer engine's final year, all 911 models feature Porsche's latest normally aspirated 3.6-liter, air-cooled, horizontally opposed, six-cylinder, 282 brake horsepower boxer engine. Redesigned in 1995, the venerable Porsche engine has a 9 percent increase in power without any fuel economy penalty, while meeting stringent international emission standards. The additional increase in horsepower, with a substantial boost in the engine's midrange torque curve, has been achieved by the incorporation of Porsche's patented Varioram induction system.

Varioram optimizes the engine's volumetric efficiency for high torque output, resulting in quick throttle response and strong acceleration. This is accomplished through the use of separate, differently tuned air intake systems for medium and high engine speeds, thus optimizing torque and power output characteristics across the usable engine rpm range. The improved engine uses inlet valves that are larger, 50 millimeters compared to 49 millimeters, and exhaust valves that are 43.5 millimeters instead of 42.5 millimeters. The camshafts have modified valve timing, and an optimized ignition system has been adopted.

The Varioram system's intake manifold operates with long intake pipes at moderate engine speeds. Cylinder filling is improved by resonance in the individual intake pipes, thus a significant increase in torque at moderate engine speeds across a relatively wide rpm range results.

A set of sliding sleeves that form part of the long intake pipes uncover apertures, located approximately at their centers, at en-

The 1998 Carrera Targa is the final evolution of the original Targa body style introduced 33 years ago. The new version does away with the removable roof panel and traditional Targa bar, replacing them with a sliding glass roof that retracts under the backlight to provide complete open-air motoring at the touch of a button. The Targa is also offered with Porsche's advanced Tiptronic S transmission, which allows manual gear shifts from a Formula One-style toggle on the steering wheel. *Porsche AG*

gine speeds over 5,000 rpm. This reduces the effective length of the intake pipes and establishes a connection with the resonance compartments. The alternating intake cycles in the left-hand and right-hand cylinder banks force the air column in the intake manifold to oscillate, or resonate, the first achieving optimum torque at the top end of the engine speed range, while resonance charging achieves optimum effect over a narrower rpm range.

The Varioram resonance system is designed to change over quickly. From 5,800 rpm up, a resonance flap opens, exposing another resonance cross-section between the resonance compartments of the two cylinder banks. The intake manifold's resonant frequency is then optimized for very high engine speeds. Combining ram effect charging and resonance charging, a combination unique to the Varioram intake manifold, high torque is produced across the entire engine speed range. Torque is improved by 18 percent at midrange engine speeds between 2,500 and 4,500 rpm. A peak output of 229 lb-ft of torque is achieved at 3,500 rpm, compared with 193 lb-ft on the earlier engine design. The torque gain is reflected in the acceleration time from 50 miles per hour to 75 miles per hour in fifth gear, which has been reduced by about 18 percent. With Varioram in place, it is possible to drive in a higher gear and with lower engine speeds with no loss in engine flexibility.

Engine output with Varioram has increased from 270 brake horsepower to 282 brake horsepower, and maximum torque from 243 lb-ft to 250 lb-ft. The high specific output and exceptional pulling power of the 3.6-liter Varioram engine make the best of everyday driving with the added benefit of lower fuel consumption.

A monitoring system for all components with exhaust emission control relevance is a feature of all 1998 Porsche 911 engines. Any time the car is driven, the OBD II (on-board diagnostics, second-generation) system measures the efficiency of the catalytic converter, identifies misfiring, and monitors the fuel system, fuel tank venting, secondary-air injection, oxygen sensors, and other components and systems that affect exhaust emissions.

Delivering output to the rear wheels, Porsche offers two transmissions for the 911 series: a standard six-speed manual and the patented Tiptronic S automatic with computer-programmed shifting and steering wheel-mounted remote shift for spirited manual gear selection. Based on Formula One–style racing transmissions, the Tiptronic steering wheel toggles allow for quickly activated gear change without the need of a clutch or removing your foot from the accelerator. Hands stay on the wheel and eyes on the road.

In addition to the 911 models, Porsche offers the new Boxster, introduced in early 1997, with its 2.5-liter water-cooled boxer engine, five-speed manual or Tiptronic S transmission. In both convertible and optional hardtop configurations, the Boxster points the way to the 911's future as the foundation for the all-new 1999 911 series.

For the 1998 model year, the new Boxster roadster will offer standard front and side air bags, but is otherwise unchanged from the 1997 model.

All Porsche 911 models and the Boxster will offer optional child seats that can automatically disable the passenger air bag system for greater child safety.

The Carrera Cabriolet offers many of the same features as the C4, without all-wheel drive. One big advantage is that the stylish 911 Cabriolet can be equipped with the advanced Tiptronic S transmission, which is particularly desirable for owners who do a great deal of city driving.

All of the roadholding stability of the all-wheel-drive Carrera 4 and the open-air luxury of the 911 Cabriolet are combined in the stunning Carrera 4 Cabriolet. Powered by Porsche's latest normally aspirated 3.6-liter, air-cooled, horizontally opposed, six-cylinder, 282-brake horsepower engine working in concert with second-generation Carrera 4 all-wheel-drive technology, the C4 Cabriolet is the most performance-oriented open car in Porsche's production history.

Based on Formula One style racing transmissions, the Tiptronic steering wheel toggles allow for quick gear change without the need of a clutch or removing your foot from the accelerator. The Tiptronic S control unit features five adaptive shift programs, which are applied according to the needs of the driver, with a range extending from economy to performance. The Tiptronic makes decisions in choosing the right gear based on vehicle and driver behavior. If the driver suddenly takes his or her foot off the accelerator, the Tiptronic S system senses the car is no longer under power and will prevent the transmission from shifting up, keeping the current gear engaged. Brake application will likewise make the transmission shift down at an appropriate road speed. Tiptronic S allows a driver to participate in shifting decisions, choosing the gears as appropriate. Once selection of the manual mode is made, shifting can be done either by using the upshift and downshift toggles on the steering wheel, as on Formula One racing cars, or by using the floor shifter, pushing forward (+) for a higher gear or pulling back (-) for a lower gear.

The open car is still the foundation of the Porsche line, as it has been since the 356 models were introduced 50 years ago. The latest Porsche convertible, the 911 Carrera 4 Cabriolet, continues that tradition by combining the enjoyment of open-air motoring with the traction and roadholding of Porsche's C4 all-wheel-drive system. Key features include the 3.6-liter flat-six 282-horsepower engine, six-speed manual transmission, all-wheel-drive, high-performance all-disc brakes with ABS, high-performance tires on alloy wheels, welded unitized body of double-sided galvanized steel, aluminum suspension components, speed-dependent extendable rear spoiler, second-generation side-impact protection, heated windshield washer nozzles, fog lamps incorporated into the front spoiler, and modular polyellipsoid headlamps with a headlamp washer system. Optional are Litronic gas-discharge headlamps, which are twice as powerful as halogen headlamps while using 30 percent less electrical current.

Modifications to the six-speed manual transmission have made the Porsche 911 Carrera 4 Cabriolet more enjoyable to drive in everyday conditions. Dual-cone synchronizers for first and second gears, along with ball-bearing sleeves that reduce friction and enhance shift precision, are features of the manual gearbox that make shifting action more precise and driving a 911 even more pleasant.

The six-speed transmission weighs virtually the same as the previous five-speed version. Weight savings coupled with operating efficiencies were design parameters throughout development of the Porsche Carrera 4 Cabriolet. (The Tiptronic S automatic transmission is not available on the Carrera 4 Cabriolet.)

The same all-wheel-drive system used on the 1997 Porsche 911 Turbo is used on the 1998 Carrera 4 Cabriolet. At 111 pounds, the system is half the weight of the earlier Carrera 4 all-wheel-drive system and is 33 percent more efficient in operation. A maintenance-free viscous center-clutch controls power distribution between the front and rear wheels. The viscous clutch, which runs in silicone fluid, responds to power and engine speed differences to vary the amount of slip between the front and rear axles.

If both rear wheels spin, the center clutch diverts engine power to the front wheels, ensuring that maximum traction is always available. Torque split between the rear wheels is regulated by a conventional rear locking differential. The viscous clutch and rear differential act together to divert engine torque to the wheels with the most traction.

Porsche's Automatic Brake Differential (ABD) system augments rear differential action. Should one rear wheel begin to spin, the locking differential transmits the power to the other wheel, which still has traction. If this is not sufficient to restore traction, then ABD, using input from the antilock brake system sensors, applies braking power to the slipping wheel to help initiate traction. The ABD system functions at speeds up to 43 miles per hour.

The three-way combination of locking differential, ABD, and all-wheel drive provides greater directional stability and offers maximum traction on less-than-ideal road surfaces. All-wheel drive reduces weight transfer differences, which can affect stability, by allowing the maximum of the Carrera 4 Cabriolet's weight to be used at all times to help maintain traction. This ideal arrangement makes the 1998 models the best handling and most predictable cars in the company's history.

The Carrera 4 Cabriolet front suspension is an evolution of the MacPherson-type strut, coil spring, and stabilizer bar unit from past 911 models that provides increased stability, excellent handling, and a comfortable ride. Due to design changes made to most suspension components, the suspension system weighs some 6.6 pounds less than its predecessor, thus improving driving characteristics by reducing unsprung weight.

The 993 series' Lightweight-Stable-Agile (LSA) multilink, subframe-mounted rear suspension system has replaced the semi-trailing arms and struts of previous 911 models. Four lateral links in two horizontal planes, which appear like upper and lower A-arms, provide precise wheel control. A refined version of the "Weissach" suspension pioneered on the Porsche 928 helps improve stability by using the outside rear wheel toe-in during cornering. Stability, regardless of side forces, and precise tracking are the system's virtues. The LSA package, in addition to the four links, includes dual gas shock absorbers, coil springs, and a rear-mounted forged aluminum subframe.

Porsche cars have made their reputation on their braking as well as their acceleration and cornering, and the 1998 Carrera 4 Cabriolet carries on that tradition. The Carrera 4 Cabriolet and all other 911 variants use large-diameter, internally vented, and cross-drilled rotors, four-piston calipers, and asbestos-free brake pads, augmented by the Bosch ABS 5 antilock braking system.

The Carrera 4 Cabriolet comes equipped with 17-inch pressure-cast alloy wheels (7Jx17 inches in the front and 9Jx17 inches in the rear) fitted with steel-belted radial 205/50 ZR-17 tires up front and 255/40 ZR-17 in the rear.

The Carrera 4 Cabriolet has a fully lined and padded power-operated convertible top with automatic latching and unlatching. The convertible top is designed to operate quickly, quietly, and safely. (The top can only be raised or lowered when the car is stopped and the parking brake is set.) A rocker switch on the center console operates the electric top mechanism, and a folding cover is provided to secure the convertible top when it is in the down position.

The Carrera 4 Cabriolet interior features Porsche's 2+2 leather seating package with power height adjustment (optional full electrical adjustment) and a white-on-black instrument panel including five round analog gauges, with the traditional ignition switch to the left of the steering wheel. Carrera 4 Cabriolet interior equipment includes dual front airbags, three-point restraints

for driver and passengers, automatic temperature control air conditioning, power windows, central locking and alarm system with immobilizer and remote entry system, heated external rearview mirrors, leather-covered steering wheel, interior lights with delayed shut off, cruise control, cassette/coin holder, and door trim panels with covered armrest bins and open map pockets.

A six-speaker AM/FM cassette audio system manufactured by Becker is standard on the Carrera 4 Cabriolet. System features include a head unit with removable control panel (for security), electronic tuning, and digital display. Available options include an in-dash compact disc player, a remote CD changer, an eight-speaker 150-watt audio system, and digital signal processing.

Other significant options available for the Porsche 911 Carrera 4 Cabriolet are full-power leather sport seats, Litronic high-intensity discharge headlamps, a rear-seat delete package, infrared security system, and limited-slip differential with automatic brake differential (ABD).

Designed for those drivers who want Porsche's legendary acceleration, braking, and handling performance combined with the joys of open-air motoring in a traditional rear-wheel-drive configuration, the Porsche 911 Carrera Cabriolet combines the structural strength of a 911 Coupe with a high-performance convertible top system and can be ordered with either the six-speed manual or the four-speed Tiptronic S automatic transmission.

The Cabriolet comes equipped with 16-inch pressure cast alloy wheels (7Jx16 inches front and 9Jx16 inches rear) fitted with steel-belted radial 205/55 ZR-16 tires up front and 245/45 ZR-16 rear. Targa-style 17-inch pressure-cast alloy wheels and Turbo-look 18-inch pressure-cast alloy wheels, both with wheel locks, are optional on the Cabriolet for 1998.

The Carrera Cabriolet has the same options as the Carrera 4 Cabriolet and comes standard with a six-speaker AM/FM cassette audio system manufactured by Becker.

The familiar 911 silhouette is evident in the 1998 Carrera S and incorporates all the aerodynamic and safety refinements made to the 911. The Carrera S has all of the same key features as the Cabriolet but can be ordered with either a six-speed manual or the four-speed Tiptronic S automatic transmission.

The Tiptronic S control unit features five different adaptive shift programs, which are applied according to the needs of the driver with a range extending from economy to performance.

The Tiptronic S electronic transmission makes decisions in choosing the right gear based on vehicle and driver behavior. If the driver suddenly takes his or her foot off the accelerator, the Tiptronic S system senses the car is no longer under power, and it will prevent the transmission from shifting up, keeping the current gear engaged. Brake application will likewise make the transmission shift down at an appropriate road speed. Built-in grade detection prevents the transmission from upshifting too soon on uphill and downhill grades. If the wheels should spin on a low-traction surface, the Tiptronic S will upshift earlier, providing engine torque management and enhanced driving stability.

Tiptronic S allows a driver to participate in shifting decisions, choosing the four gears as appropriate. Transmission control on the 911 Carrera S includes the choice of manual or automatic mode, depending on the position of the selector lever. Once selection of the manual mode is made, shifting can be done either by using the upshift and downshift buttons on the steering wheel, as on Formula One racing cars, or by using the floor shifter, pushing forward for a higher gear, or pulling back for a lower gear. A six-function computerized driver information center is included on Carrera S models equipped with the optional Tiptronic S transmission.

The Carrera S comes equipped with special "Cup Design" 17-inch pressure-cast alloy wheels incorporating colored Porsche crest wheel caps (7Jx17 inches in the front and 9Jx17 inches in the rear) fitted with steel-belted radial 205/50 ZR-17 tires up front and 255/40 ZR-17 rear tires. Targa-style 17-inch pressure-cast alloy wheels and hollow-spoke 18-inch pressure-cast alloy wheels, both with wheel locks, are optional on the Carrera S.

Special Carrera S interior equipment includes black leather and steel gray interior trim, steel gray doorsill panels, instrument rings, shift lever knob, hand brake lever and push knob, a textured black leather dashboard center and door panels, along with dual front airbags, three-point restraints for driver and passengers, automatic temperature-control air conditioning, power windows, electronic sunroof, central locking and alarm system with immobilizer and remote entry system, heated external rearview mirrors, individually folding rear seatbacks, leather-covered steering wheel, interior lights with delayed shut off, cruise control, cassette/coin holder and door trim panels with covered armrest bins, and open map pockets.

The Becker six-speaker AM/FM cassette audio system is also standard on the Carrera S. Available options are the Tiptronic S automatic transmission, full-power leather sport seats, Litronic high-intensity discharge headlamps, sport chassis (with larger front and rear stabilizer bars, stiffer springs, specially tuned front and rear shock absorbers), a rear-seat delete package, infrared security system, and limited-slip differential with automatic brake differential (ABD).

The 1998 Carrera 4S combines the widebody exterior design of the famed 911 Turbo and the Turbo's all-wheel-drive system with the normally aspirated 911 engine and six-speed manual transmission. The Tiptronic S automatic transmission is not available.

Included with the Carrera 4S are Turbo-look 18-inch pressure-cast alloy wheels and the same power-assisted, internally vented, four-piston disc brakes used on the 911 Turbo. The

Carrera 4S six-speed manual gearbox is optimized for smooth, light, and precise shifting.

The side rocker panels and wider rear fenders of the Carrera 4S were adapted from the widebody design used on the 1997 Porsche 911 Turbo. The Carrera 4S, like the legendary Turbo, has a front air dam with large air intakes to provide additional cooling air for the engine and auxiliary equipment. Rather than the Turbo tail, the Carrera 4S has a speed-dependent, extendible rear spoiler identical to other 911 models.

The same all-wheel-drive system used on the 1997 Porsche 911 Turbo is used on the 1998 Carrera 4S Coupe. The three-way combination of locking differential, ABD, and all-wheel drive provides the C4S with greater directional stability and maximum traction.

Interior features of the Carrera 4S are the same as the C4 Cabriolet. Electronic sunroof, central locking and alarm system with immobilizer, and remote entry system are also standard features. A six-speaker AM/FM cassette audio system manufactured by Becker is standard on the Carrera 4S. Options include full-power leather sport seats, Litronic high-intensity discharge headlamps, sport chassis (with larger front and rear stabilizer bars, stiffer springs, specially tuned front and rear shock absorbers), a rear-seat delete package, infrared security system, and limited-slip differential with automatic brake differential (ABD).

The final model of the 911 series is the revised Targa introduced in 1996, which features a unique electric sliding glass roof system with sun visor and separate wind deflector, in place of the original Targa roof design and removable panel. Nearly the entire roof over the passenger compartment slides down and back to its stowed position under the rear window, providing an open-air feeling much greater than that of the original 911 Targa.

The tinted privacy glass, specially treated to block out 100 percent of ultraviolet rays, slides back quietly and smoothly at the touch of a button and can be stopped anywhere throughout its entire range of motion.

Below the window line the Targa shares its body and platform with the 911 Carrera Cabriolet, including additional body and chassis reinforcements for increased structural rigidity. The roof module, which resembles the Coupe roof in profile, consists of two-layer laminated safety glass, a sun visor, a wind deflector, a rear window, and an aluminum frame.

The Targa was designed to provide several advantages over the original design, including minimal noise, maximum operating convenience, and no undesirable drafts or turbulence in the passenger compartment with the roof open. The Targa's roof contour offers nearly the same amount of headroom in the rear seats as the Coupe, even with the roof open, and slightly more front seat headroom than the Coupe when the roof is closed. No unpleasant drafts of air occur in the passenger compartment,

Closer to its roots than any other model, the 1998 Carrera S is Porsche's "basic" 911 and can be ordered with either a six-speed manual or the four-speed Tiptronic S automatic transmission. The Carrera S comes equipped with special "Cup Design" 17-inch pressure-cast alloy wheels incorporating colored Porsche crest wheel caps. The optional sport chassis (with larger front and rear stabilizer bars, stiffer springs, specially tuned front and rear shock absorbers), a rear-seat delete package, infrared security system, and limited-slip differential with automatic brake differential (ABD) are available to turn the Carrera S into a sports racing model.

even when traveling at high speeds with the roof open. The interior noise level is quieter inside the open-top Targa than in a Carrera Cabriolet or a Coupe with a sliding sunroof and the Targa roof can be opened or closed while the car is moving.

The tinted glass roof lends a new feel to driving when it is closed, and the wide field of vision creates a sense of greater interior space, giving the impression of open-top driving even when the Targa roof is closed.

According to temperature measurements taken in bright sunlight, the Targa interior does not heat up more than the Coupe. Thanks to the design of the water deflection system integrated into the glass roof's seals, opening the roof after traveling through rain is no problem. Water flowing off the panel is prevented from dripping inside the car.

The Targa roof is brought into position as a complete module and joined permanently to the body during final assembly. The main components of the roof module are the strong side posts, which are joined together by cross-members. The rear window of single-plate laminated glass is bonded together with the sheet metal structure. The wind deflector and glass-panel sunroof are made of 7-millimeter-thick laminated glass

consisting of two panes of glass 3 millimeters thick and several layers of plastic film.

Including the extra-thick glass, three electric motors, a longer rear window wiper, the roller blind and wind deflector, the Targa weighs some 66 pounds more than a standard 911 Carrera, and the strong roof structure provides safety and torsional rigidity. The built-on roof module lends the 911 Targa a distinctive look.

The 1998 Porsche 911 Targa comes equipped with its own special Targa-style 17-inch pressure-cast alloy wheels (7Jx17 inches in the front and 9Jx17 inches in the rear) fitted with steel-belted radial 205/50 ZR-17 tires up front and 255/40 ZR-17 in the rear.

The car can be ordered with either a six-speed manual or the four-speed Tiptronic S automatic transmission along with full-power leather sport seats, Litronic high-intensity discharge headlamps, a rear-seat delete package, infrared security system, and limited-slip differential with automatic brake differential (ABD).

Of all the 911 models, the Targa represents the highest tier of design evolution, the final 911 as we know it.

But this is not the end of the 911.

CHAPTER NINE

996

911 for the Next Millennium

A longer wheelbase makes the 996 the largest 911 ever, with more interior room for driver and passenger. The rear seating also benefits but is still consigned to short trips and best suited for children, pets, or packages. The car's profile and new windshield rake give the 996 a sleeker, more sweptback look than its 993 predecessor. *Porsche AG*

Despite its smaller displacement, the all-new 911 Carrera six engine delivers 14 brake horsepower more than the old air-cooled 993 engine it replaces. Nearly 3 inches shorter and almost 5 inches lower than its predecessor, the new water-cooled boxer engine is similar, but not identical, to the 2.5-liter engine used in the Boxster. Engine capacity of the new Carrera is 3.4 liters (3,387 cc) versus 3.6 liters for the 993. Cylinder bore and stroke is 96x78 millimeters (3.78x3.07 inches), with an 11.3:1 compression ratio. *Porche AG*

In September 1997, Porsche introduced the next-generation 911 at the Frankfurt auto show. The new 911, designated as the Type 996, replaces the 993 at the end of 1998 model year production for the North American market and a year earlier for the European market. The new 911 models will be built alongside the Boxster, upon which much of the 996's design is based.

From the front, the 996 is almost identical to the Boxster. The profile is still representative of the famous 911 shape; however, the rear shows a great influence from the 928 and turns down in half the distance of the old 911 for the shortest rear overhang ever.

The rear wing is also new in design and deploys at 75 miles per hour rather than 48 miles per hour, as on the previous Carrera line.

The new models are taller than their predecessors, with a roofline that crests above the driver's head, rather than at the windshield as on the 993 series. The windshield is also more steeply raked at 60 degrees versus 55 degrees for the 993.

Wheelbase is 3.2 inches longer at 92.6 inches and 7.3 inches greater in overall length. Most of that added length is gained in interior space, approximately 6.7 inches, according to Porsche. The car is also 1.2 inches wider, which means more interior room for shoulders, arms, and legs.

The interior is completely new, the first total redesign in 35 years. From the instrument panel to the doors, every inch of the new 911 starts with a fresh sheet of paper—with the exception of the ignition switch, which is still to the left of the steering wheel!

The most significant change for 1999 is the engine, the first water-cooled, six-cylinder boxer engine ever to power a production 911. Similar in design to the 2.5-liter Boxster engine, the new 911 Carrera six has a displacement of 3.4 liters.

On the whole, this is a far better car than any previous 911, and yes, it is still a 911 despite the sacrilege of a water-cooled engine. It is just a boxer on a liquid diet.

Under the rear deck lid, the 911's new water-cooled flat-six puts out 14 brake horsepower more than the old engine (300 brake horsepower at 6,800 rpm, torque at 258 lb-ft at 4,600 rpm), despite its smaller displacement. Nearly 3 inches shorter and almost 5 inches lower than its predecessor, the Carrera engine is similar to, but not identical with, the Boxster's powerplant. Engine capacity of the new Carrera is 3,387 cc, or 3.4 versus 3.6 liters for the 993. The 996 engine comes with an extra-short stroke in the interest of high revs and superior running refinement. Cylinder bore and stroke is 96x78 millimeters (3.78x3.07 inches). The compression ratio is very high at 11.3:1, ensuring maximum power and minimum consumption when running on premium-plus fuel. The electronic engine management comes complete with antiknock control allowing far more power than the Boxster, even on low-grade fuel, thanks to the larger engine capacity.

The 996 has a two-piece engine block made of pressure-cast light alloy, and the wear-proof cylinder liners made of an aluminum/silicon alloy are cast into position. The crankshaft runs in a separate support reinforced by cast steel and even stronger in its design and structure than on the Boxster. The camshafts are driven by an auxiliary shaft and chains with automatic tightening. The four valves per cylinder, in turn, are operated by a total of four overhead camshafts. The intake camshaft is adjusted automatically by 25 degrees for optimum performance at all speeds. A variable intake manifold with adjustable volume serves to further improve the cylinder charge and engine torque. The oil sump is in a special chamber beneath the

For the first time in 35 years, Porsche has completely redesigned the 911 interior. All that remains of the original design is the ignition switch, still in the traditional position, to the left of the steering column. *Porsche AG*

There's more than a passing resemblance to the Boxster in the front of the 996. In fact, it's identical. A sharing of design and engineering, as well as assembly lines, ties the smaller, two-seat sport model closely to the 996. The new headlight design used on both cars gives Porsche an all-new, immediately recognizable brand identity. *Porsche AG*

With improved aerodynamics and a new water-cooled boxer engine delivering 300 brake horsepower, the all-new Porsche 911 Carrera is the highest performance base model in the car's history. The Carrera Coupe will be the first 996 available, followed shortly by a Cabriolet version. The cars go on sale in Germany for the 1998 model year and in Spring 1998 as 1999 models in North America. *Porsche AG*

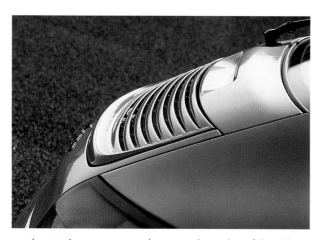

The 996 has an integrated wing similar to that of the older 993, although, this one does not deploy until the car reaches 75 miles per hour, rather than 48 miles per hour, as on the previous Carrera line. *Porsche AG*

The lines of the 996 clearly combine the best attributes of Porsche's greatest models. The new rear fender, taillight, and bumper combination bear strong ties to that of the late front-engine 928 series, yet another brand identity that continues the distinctive styling that has become a Porsche trademark. *Porsche AG*

From any perspective, this is genuinely a 911. That it may sound slightly different, ride a bit more comfortably, and be uncommonly quiet for a Porsche is just the next step forward in an evolutionary design that once again has defied obsolescence. *Porsche AG*

crankcase, introducing a principle referred to by Porsche's engineers as integrated dry sump lubrication.

Like the Boxster, the Carrera six is fitted with Variocam, Porsche's variable valve timing system. The 911 is also equipped with Varioram, Porsche's variable intake system, although this new version differs from the previous 993 design in that it uses fixed rather than sliding intake tubes.

Because of precise control of ignition and fuel metering, the new engine delivers 10 percent greater fuel economy than the previous boxer engine and produces lower emissions. The car is also 110 pounds lighter than the 993, at 2,911 pounds.

Virtually everything on the 996 is new, even the Getrag-built six-speed manual gearbox, which was redesigned to accommodate the new engine's increased horsepower and torque. The ZF-built five-speed Tiptronic automatic has also been upgraded to match the 996 engine's greater output. The Carrera also employs a Boxster-based, cable-actuated shift mechanism that is designed to eliminate some of the alignment problems that were inherent in the old Carrera's rod-actuated linkage.

Transmission ratios	Manual	Tiptronic S
1st gear	3.82	3.66
2nd gear	2.20	2.0
3rd gear	1.52	1.41
4th gear	1.22	1.0
5th gear	1.02	0.74
6th gear	0.84	-
Reverse	3.55	4.10
Final drive ratio:	3.44	3.676

The car's longer wheelbase and wider track will undoubtedly enhance stability, especially at maximum speed, which the Porsche factory claims to be 174 miles per hour. Though the ride is typical of 911 suspension design, the new Carrera feels a bit more compliant, not so as to detract from handling, which is even better than the 993's, but to add a more luxurious feel to the highway ride. Dare we say, more like that of the late 928 GTS. And this is not at all a surprise, since the new rear suspension is derived from the former flagship V-8 model.

The suspension of the 996 is characterized in particular by the front axle jointly developed for the Boxster and Carrera. The 996 and Boxster use a McPherson design optimized by Porsche: a spring-strut axle with independent suspension on track control arms, longitudinal links and spring struts, cone base springs with inner damper, and twin-sleeve gas-pressure dampers.

The McPherson-design track control arms and longitudinal links on the front axle are connected elastically to one another, providing elastokinematic effects stabilizing the car's driving behavior. The modified front end geometry also provides space for the rack-and-pinion steering to now be mounted ahead of the front axle, allowing even better steering.

The rear is a multilink axle with independent suspension on five-track control arms/links, cylindrical coil springs on each wheel with co-axial inner damper, and single-sleeve gas-pressure dampers. In the interest of driving safety, toe-in is corrected elastokinematically as on the Porsche 928's "Weissach" axle.

The diameter of the aluminum rims for the 996 has been increased to 17 inches on the standard model with 205/50 and 255/40 Z-rated tires. The sports suspension features 18-inch wheels surrounded by 225/40 and 265/35 tires.

There will be five versions of the new 911, including the Targa, which will be a continuation of the 993 Series, equipped with the traditional air-cooled six-cylinder horizontally opposed engine. The 3.6 will deliver 285 brake horsepower at 6,100 rpm, with a maximum torque of 251 lb-ft at 5,250 rpm. Targas will be available with the older six-speed manual gearbox or the 993 four-speed Tiptronic S automatic transmission.

The all-new design of the body structure, as well as the use of extra-strong steel panels at all highly exposed points, serves to enhance passive safety to a standard never seen before. Improved crash integrity in a head-on collision significantly reduces the occupants' risk of injury. In side impacts the driver and passenger are also better protected than ever before, as Porsche once again sets new standards in terms of enhanced passive safety with the introduction of the revolutionary POSIP system. An acronym for Porsche Side Impact Protection, POSIP offers sidebags in a new, innovative design giving both driver and passenger greater and more comprehensive safety. POSIP uses two sidebags, which are not emptied immediately after inflation and offer their full protective effect in an open convertible, which makes them unique. A further distinction is that the sidebag modules fitted in the door panels provide a particularly large volume when inflated. Expanding to a total capacity of 30 liters, or 1.05 cubic feet, these extra-large sidebags ensure not only the usual protection at shoulder level, but cushion your entire body from the hips to the head. This superior safety is ensured by POSIP through the above-average capacity of the sidebags, regardless of the fore-and-aft position of the seat.

The sidebags are inflated by a hybrid gas generator, with the use of pyrotechnical systems being restricted to a minimum. The two sidebags are activated in a collision by a sensor in the side-sill beneath the door. Both the 911 Carrera and the Boxster are available with the POSIP safety system.

That's a lot of changes for one car, and the question arises, "Is it still a 911, or isn't it?" Only time will tell, but from first impressions, it is no more than another step in the car's evolution. To quote Porsche AG, "A new Porsche simply has the commitment to redefine the state of the art. And this time Porsche's engineers in Weissach have gone a particularly long way to achieve such outstanding progress. For the new six-cylinder horizontally opposed power unit was required to outperform its predecessor—after 35 years of outstanding success—in terms of engine output, performance, refinement, economy, and environmental compatibility. And at the same time driving dynamics were to be improved to the highest level. Retaining its classic lines, the body was intended to offer extra space, enhanced structural stiffness, even greater passive safety, and, at the same time, less weight."

Maybe it's not the car Porsche enthusiasts have lusted after for 35 years, but—no matter how many new features the 996 incorporates—it is still the definitive 911, a car that neither time, nor Porsche, can truly change.

APPENDIX

ANATOMY OF A 911

Throughout its 35-year history the 911 has been completely redesigned several times over, yet its basic shape and engineering have remained intact, a contradiction that has perplexed automakers and enthusiasts the world over for decades, while earning the 911 a reputation as the most revered sports car of its time.

The 911 has always been a simple, straightforward idea, and perhaps that has been the secret of its longevity. No matter how many times the engineers and stylists at Zuffenhausen and Weissach have improved upon the car, they have never forsaken the basic canons of the 911 design.

Here is a chronology of change, beginning with the 901 prototype and evolving through 35 years of 911 production to highlight improvements in engine, transmission, suspension, and body design. A road map, if you will, from Zuffenhausen in 1963 to the last 993 models of 1998.

THE 901/911 PROTOTYPES

Before the 911 went into production in November 1964, a total of 13 901/911 prototypes were built, with chassis numbers 13 321 to 13 333. Numbers 13 330 and 13 331 were predecessors of the four-cylinder 912. Although based on the same design no two 901/911 prototypes were alike. They were used for display purposes as well as testing, underwent continuous modification, and differed from later production cars in many details. The Frankfurt International Automobile Show (IAA) in September 1963 marked the official birth of the 911.

Technical
Engine

The six-cylinder boxer engine was developed in early 1960, under type designation 745. This version still employed pushrods, four main bearings, and two axial cooling blowers driven by fan belts from the crankshaft. The next development stage was designated Type 821 and closely resembled the later production engine. The main difference was that this type did not employ dry sump lubrication. It

had also been decided that the use of pushrod engines was to be discontinued.

Fuel and Ignition Systems

Even the early Type 745 engine relied on downdraft Solex carburetors for its supply of air-fuel mixture. Before the production 40 PI carburetors were ready, Porsche conducted its tests with a Solex application used for Lancias, the Type 40 PBIC.

Powertrain

It was decided early on that the 911 would be best suited to a five-speed manual transmission. The gearbox was considered for its use in competition as well. To provide a shift pattern that would also be suitable for racing, first gear was located to the left and back, reverse gear left and forward. Development of the new transmission was relatively free of problems; as inventor of the blocking synchromesh system, Porsche had access to enormous technical expertise.

Suspension

Porsche had already experimented with a new suspension design on the 356. Both 901 prototypes were still fitted with front subframes and 356 rear suspensions. Prior to production, it was decided to use a new suspension system at the rear.

Bodywork

The first renderings, carrying the designation Type 695, were done in 1957, largely by independent designer Albrecht Goertz. Butzi Porsche created the Type 754 T7 in 1959, with a slight break in the roofline between the backlight and engine lid. A rather overloaded design, Type 754 T9, was drawn by Porsche's chief of body engineering, Erwin Komenda. The 901 was eventually developed from Butzi Porsche's design. The prototypes had no bumper guards or side deco strips, but had dual exhaust outlets. The location of the windshield wiper arms was the subject of extensive discussions. Early versions had their wipers parked on the right to provide a larger field of view.

Equipment

The new Porsche had large glass areas—a genuine 2+2, with fold-down rear seatbacks like its predecessor. In the beginning, two large round instruments were employed; the combination of five round instruments with green faces was not completed until 1964. The interior of the prototype shown at the 1963 IAA differed greatly from the later production version.

Seats and Trim

Porsche intended to offer the new model with a full leather interior as standard equipment, but in fact leatherette was combined with fabric, usually in a houndstooth or herringbone pattern. Porsche placed great emphasis on a comfortable seat position for its sporty Grand Touring car. The seats were produced by Recaro GmbH and Company, which had evolved out of the coachbuilding division of Karosseriewerk Reutter, purchased by Porsche AG in July 1963.

Heating System

Because the heating system was engine speed and load dependent, tests were conducted with an auxiliary heater on several of the prototypes and various cutouts under the hood can be seen on 901 experimental cars where engineers tried different systems. An auxiliary heater was later available as an option on the 911, mounted in a well in the right side of the trunk ahead of the dashboard. Originally, the battery was to be mounted in this well. Initially, the prototypes did not have a heating system, as heat exchangers were not ready until much later. For this reason, some versions had only an auxiliary heater-mounted in the trunk.

Electrical System

Early in the development of the 901/911, Porsche decided to install a high-output 12-volt system. Prototypes still used 360-watt generators.

This, then, was the initial design of the 901/911 as shown at the motor shows in 1964. As the cars neared final production, Porsche began to fine-tune the engineering and with the first production models delivered in 1965, the design of the 911 took final shape.

1965 TYPE 911

The six-cylinder, flat-opposed, single overhead cam boxer engine was introduced with a displacement of 1,991 cc. Bore and stroke were 80 millimeters x 66 millimeters with 9.0:1 compression for an output of 130 brake horsepower at 6,100 rpm. The engine was an eight-main bearing design with one camshaft per cylinder bank and camshaft drive via two timing chains. A dry sump design,

the 911 engine had the potential for racing from the time of its introduction.

Initially, the cars were delivered with six Solex PI overflow carburetors. As these proved to be difficult to synchronize, the twin banks of Solex carbs were a short-lived solution to fuel management.

Specifications

The production car suspension was independent front with struts and lateral arms; rear, independent on trailing arms. Rear drive was by means of jointed halfshafts. Front springing was by means of separate longitudinal torsion bars for each wheel. At the rear, there was one transverse round torsion bar per wheel. Shock absorbers were the front double-acting telescoping type. Toe-in and track were not adjustable in the first model year. It had ZF rack and pinion steering. The wheels were the slotted disc style, chrome plating was optional, and they had 4 1/2 Jx15 with 165 HR 15 tires. Brakes were single-circuit hydraulics with 282-millimeter front discs and 285-millimeter rear discs[Dennis: Is this correct? the front brakes were smaller than the rear?] A mechanical drum parking brake acted on both rear wheels.

Production cars featured wood veneer on the dashboard and had wood rim steering wheels.

1966 TYPE 911

Changes for 1966 included the use of Weber IDA 3L and 3C1 carburetors by midyear. Engine designations were 901/01 and 901/05 for the 1966 911 series.

1967 TYPE 911

The first significant change for the 911 series was marked by the addition of the 911 S and the Targa body style. The high-performance 911 S model delivered 160 brake horsepower, an increase of 30 brake horsepower over the standard engine, and came equipped with tuned suspension and upgraded brakes. The 901/02 engine in the 911 S offered power increases through higher compression (9.8:1), 42-millimeter intake valves, and 38-millimeter exhaust valves. The 901/02 had soft nitrided forged-steel connecting rods, forged light alloy pistons, altered camshafts, and two springs per valve. The higher brake horsepower output was reached at 6,600 rpm. Designated the Super "911S" engine, fuel was delivered via two Weber three-barrel Type IDA (S) or 40 IDS 3C and 3C1 carburetors. The 911 S required a Research Octane rated fuel of no less than 98.

The 911S was badged as a separate model and was available with a selection of gear ratios designed for various road course competitions. The 901/02 five speed was standard. Optional gear sets were 901/51 for quicker acceleration, 901/52 for hill climbs, 901/53 known as airport gears (short course), and 902/0 Nürburgring gears.

The 911 S suspension was modified for motorsports with transverse antiroll bars front and rear, Koni shock absorbers, and ventilated brake rotors. The car came equipped with Porsche-designed Fuchs alloy deep-bed 4 1/2 x15 wheels, the first alloy wheels to be offered on the 911. The Fuchs wheel became a 911 trademark.

1968 TYPE 911 (A SERIES)

Models must now meet federal emission standards, and the 911 was equipped for the first time with exhaust emissions controls. Weissach engineers accomplished this without sacrificing performance through the use of new exhaust gas recirculation technology. The 911 T and 911 L were added to the product line, along with the Sportomatic transmission as an option on all models, including the 911 S. Koni shocks remained standard for the 911 S, while 911 T and 911 L models were equipped with Boge shock absorbers. Front antiroll bar diameter was 11 millimeters for the 911 L, 15 millimeters on the 911 S, the latter also equipped with wider 5 1/2 Jx15 Fuchs alloy wheels.

1969 TYPE 911 (B SERIES)

This was the first complete model change for the 911 series with a new, longer 2,268-millimeter wheelbase, slightly flared fenders, and Bosch mechanical fuel injection for the 911 E and 911 S. The "E" designation is the German for fuel injection, *Einspritzung*. Modifications to the engine resulted in the power output for the "S" increasing to 170 brake horsepower. Standard output for the fuel-injected boxer engine was 140 brake horsepower. The 911 T remained the only model to still use carburetors, which for 1969 were a pair of Weber 40 IDT3 C three-barrels. Other modifications to the 911 S included a change to 6 Jx15 alloy wheels and 185/70 VR 15 tires as standard equipment.

All 911 models were now equipped with a smaller circumference steering wheel with padded horn button. Door panels had larger storage pockets and the inside door latch was recessed into the armrest. To add weight to the front end and improve straight-line stability, all 911s were now equipped with two batteries (each 35 Ah) located in the front fenders.

1970 TYPE 911 (C SERIES)

The Porsche 911 began its second decade with a new 2.2-liter engine (2,196 cc) achieved through an increase in cylinder bore to 84 millimeters. Power output for the 911 S was raised again, to 180 brake horsepower at 6,500 rpm. All 911 models were equipped with a new 225-millimeter Fitchtel and Sachs clutch system. The Sportomatic was no longer available for the

911 S. Body lines remained unchanged for 1970 and the model designations continued as 911 T, 911 E, and 911 S in Coupe and Targa versions.

1971 TYPE 911 (D SERIES)

This was the first true carryover year for the 911 as no significant changes were made to any of the models. In a distinct sense, Porsche never considered the 911 a year-by-year car. Changes were made as necessary and not to coincide with new model year introductions. The demands of its clientele, more often than not, dictated improvements in performance and handling, as well as experience gained in motorsports competition, which continually improved the 911 breed.

1972 TYPE 911 (E SERIES)

For 1972 Porsche increased displacement to 2.4 liters and all engines were designed to run on regular octane fuel in order to comply with U. S. standards. The increase in displacement was achieved by altering the crankshafts to give a 70.4-millimeter stroke. Compression ratio was reduced to accommodate lower octane fuels—8.5:1 in the 911 S, 8.0:1 in the 911 E, and 7.5:1 in the 911 T, with a minimum octane rating of 91. Although compression was lower, the larger displacement resulted in increased output; 190 brake horsepower for the 911 S, 165 brake horsepower for the 911 E, and 130 brake horsepower for the 911 T. All models were equipped with the new Type 915 transmission, and limited slip differential was now available as an option. All 1972 models featured 2.4 badging on the engine air inlet grille. The 911 S was equipped with a steel front spoiler.

1973 TYPE 911 (F SERIES)

The steel front spoiler introduced in 1972 on the 911 S was made available for all 911 models. Beginning with the 911 T in January 1973, U. S. models are delivered with the new Bosch K-Jetronic fuel-injection system. A new six-cylinder model was introduced, the 911 SC (Carrera RS) available in sport and touring versions and powered by a 2.7-liter engine. In standard trim, the SC weighed 2,368 pounds, while the "Lightweight Carrera" version, with a 2.8-liter engine, weighed only 1,982 pounds. The aerodynamic Carrera RS series was the beginning of an entirely new generation of 911 models that dominated sports car club racing throughout the 1970s, culminating in the RSR 3.0.

Wheelbase for all 911 models was increased again, to 2,271 millimeters, and all 911 models returned to front torsion bar equipment. Hydropneumatic front struts, previously standard on the 911 E, were now available as options for the T, E, and S. The Carrera RS became the top performance model in the 911 line, relegating the 911 S to second position.

1974 TYPE 911 (G SERIES)

The 911 became more Americanized in 1974 as Weissach re-engineered the car to meet U. S. safety standards, which again became more stringent for imported cars. To meet new 5-mile-per-hour crash standards, both bumpers were completely redesigned, in turn altering the front and rear shape of the 911 for the first time since its introduction. Front turn signals were integrated into the bumpers, which were now painted in body color and fitted with wraparound rubber trim strips.

All models were fitted with a 2,687-cc engine, once again increasing output to 210 brake horsepower for the 911 SC, 175 brake horsepower for the 911 S, and 150 brake horsepower for the 911. The Carrera RS remained a separate model with a 3.0-liter engine; only 111 examples of this car were built.

1975 TYPE 911 (H SERIES)

The 911, 911 S, and 911 Carrera Coupe and Targa were carried over for the 1975 model year and the new 911 Turbo Coupe (known as the 930) joined the model line for European sale only. A completely new four-speed manual transmission (Type 930/30) was designed exclusively for the 911 Turbo. The four-speed gearbox represented a new design necessary for the limited space and output demands of the Turbo engine. The Turbo also had a completely reworked suspension design tuned to the car's higher performance.

1976 TYPE 911 (J SERIES)

With the front-engine 924 on the market as an entry-level Porsche, only three versions of the 911 are offered in 1976: two normally aspirated models, 911 and 911 Carrera and the 911 Turbo. The 911 retained the 2.7-liter engine, while the Carrera was fitted with a 3.0-liter (2,994-cc) engine and K-Jetronic fuel-injection system. Output from the 3.0 is rated at 200 brake horsepower at 6,000 rpm, while the 2.7 delivered 165 brake horsepower at 5,800 rpm. Output from the Turbo was rated at 245 brake horsepower. The Sportomatic transmission, available only for the nonturbocharged models, was changed to a three speed (earlier versions were four speed) to meet more stringent noise standards. Structural parts of all bodies are made of hot-dip galvanized steel. There was a six-year warranty against rust perforation of the floor pan.

1977 TYPE 911 (K SERIES)

This became a carryover year for Porsche, which, considering the changes made in 1976, was not unexpected. The few improvements made for 1977 were mechanical, such as the introduction of Bosch EKP IV fuel supply pumps, easier to operate clutches, and vacuum power-assist brakes for the 911 Carrera 3.0, Turbo, and Sportomatic-equipped 911 models. Turbos were fitted with 16-inch wheels and tires, 7 Jx16 front, 8 Jx16 rear with 205/55VR 16, and 225/50 VR 16 tires, respectively.

1978 TYPE 911 (L SERIES)

Porsche reduced the number of 911 models once again and for 1978 there were only two 911 versions available, 911 SC (Coupe and Targa) and 911 Turbo 3.3. It was the first indication that the 911 might be headed for the end of the road as the new front-engined 928 became Zuffenhausen's flagship model. Porsche, however, preserved the 911's competitive edge with the new intercooled 3.3-liter Turbo maintaining a performance margin over the eight-cylinder 928. The Turbo has a completely new brake system adapted from the 917 race car using ventilated brake rotors with cross-drilled surfaces. Sturdy four-piston calipers bear the PORSCHE name, and not only add further identity to the car, but significantly enhance the Turbo's ability to scrub off top speeds in excess of 160 miles per hour.

1979 TYPE 911 (M SERIES)

This is a complete carryover year for the 911 and no significant changes are made to the SC or Turbo.

1980 TYPE 911 (A PROGRAM)

Power increased for the 911 SC to 188 horsepower. This was the first application of an oxygen sensor (*Lambda sond*) for U. S. engines. Dual exhaust tips were standard for the Turbo 3.3.

1981 TYPE 911 (B PROGRAM)

There were no significant changes to Turbo 3.3. Again, there was a power increase for the 911 SC to 204 horsepower. An antirust warranty period extended to seven years and expanded to cover the entire body. The Sportomatic transmission was discontinued.

1982 TYPE 911 (C PROGRAM)

There were only minor changes from the previous model year. The most notable change was the availability of the Turbo Tail as an option for the 911 SC. A special edition was also offered with Ferry Porsche's signature embroidered in the seat backrests.

1983 TYPE 911 (D PROGRAM)

This became a pivotal year for Porsche with the addition of the long-awaited 911 Cabriolet, a car that had been planned as far back as 1963 but never put into production. With the Cabriolet, Zuffenhausen brought the 911 full circle, and it seemed as though there was little left that Porsche could do to improve the 911. Aside from the all-new Cabriolet, there were no significant changes in the product line. The new convertible model did, however, bring about a renaissance of the open car within the sports car world. Porsche had reignited a flame that most automakers had considered long burnt out.

1984 TYPE 911 (E PROGRAM)

On the heels of the new Cabriolet, Porsche saw a resurgence in sales and entered the 1984 model year with a new 3.2-liter (3,164-cc) boxer engine. Although the Turbo was no longer available for sale in the U.S. market, as it could not as yet be equipped with a catalytic converter, the 3.3-liter model was still sold in Canada. The 911 Carrera is fitted with a more powerful brake system, and the Turbo look is offered as an option on 911 Coupes. Digital Motor Electronics (DME) is employed for the Carrera engine's fuel injection and map ignition bringing about better fuel efficiency and reduced emissions.

1985 TYPE 911 (F PROGRAM)

You still could not get a Turbo in the United States in 1985, but the Turbo look was so prevalent no one could tell. All three 911 models, Coupe, Targa, and Cabriolet were available with optional Turbo body treatments, although without the Turbo Tail (which could be ordered and installed by most aftermarket Porsche tuners in the United States). The cars were also equipped with Boge "GZ" dual-tube gas-pressurized shocks, and brakes once again were improved for reduced pedal effort. Seating was redesigned and offered power adjustments as an option.

1986 TYPE 911 (G PROGRAM)

Porsche finally sorted out the problem with catalytic converters and turbo engines and American Porsche enthusiasts got the best turbocharged 911 yet, the 930/68 developing 282 brake horsepower at 5,500 rpm. (European versions had 300 brake horsepower and significantly more torque: 430 lb-ft versus 390 lb-ft in U.S. trim. Both models achieved maximum torque at 4,000 rpm). The new 3.3-liter Turbo engine was available in all models, Coupe, Targa, and Cabriolet, for the first time, giving Porsche the most extensive line of cars ever: 911 Carrera Coupe, Targa, Cabriolet 911 Carrera Turbo Look Coupe, Targa, and Cabriolet, and the three Turbo versions. The Turbo was equipped with the four-speed 930/36 transmission. All 911 models received larger front antiroll bars (up 2 millimeters to 22 millimeters) and rear torsion bars (increased 1 millimeter to 25 millimeters). The rear antiroll bar diameter is also increased (from 18 millimeters to 21 millimeters). Porsche concluded its new option list by offering the Cabriolet with an electrically operated top.

1987 TYPE 911 (H PROGRAM)

The entire 911 model line was carried over into 1987 and the only notable change was the addition of the 911 Carrera Club Sport (Sport Package M 637). Designed for SCCA and Porsche Club competition, this was a stripped-down-for-racing version that shaved 110 pounds off the standard Carrera and tipped the scales at 2,555 pounds. The Club Sport had a higher engine rev limit, sport shocks, 7 and 8Jx17 wheels, and stiffer engine mounts.

1988 TYPE 911 (J PROGRAM)

Porsche made no major changes to the 911 series this year, with the exception of offering the Turbo in the European 935 slant-nose configuration: front bodywork with flat nose, fenders, retractable headlights, vents atop fenders, rocker panel fairings, and air inlets with strakes in the rear fenders. The special order models were produced at Zuffenhausen using galvanized steel for the *flachtbau* conversion. The very stylish racebred design propagated an entire aftermarket industry that rallied to build both steel and fiberglass versions of the slant nose retrofitted to stock 911 Turbos and Carreras.

1989 TYPE 911 (K PROGRAM)

This was to become a watershed year for Porsche with the introduction of the Carrera 4, a highly refined production version of the 959. The C4 introduced significant changes in body lines and was the only model for 1989 to feature the revised coachwork—integrated front and rear bumpers and smoother, more rounded body lines.

The new C4 engine, designated M64/01, was a 3.6-liter design delivering 250 brake horsepower. This was the first new 911 engine rated for worldwide distribution to meet all emissions and noise requirements. Compression ratio was a stout 11.3:1, and torque, 310 lb-ft, was delivered at a low 4,800 rpm. The most advanced 911 road car yet produced, the C4 redefined the performance envelope for rear-engined sports car, virtually nullifying through AWD all of the 911's negative handling characteristics. (See chapter 7.)

The 911 Carrera Coupe, Targa, Cabriolet, and Turbo retained the older design for one more year, and the old body plant was temporarily closed to retool for the C4 design, being produced in a new modern factory. The Turbo was now equipped with a five-speed transmission with closer gear ratios. The C4 became the standard 911 body style in 1990. The very last cars to feature the older Carrera coachwork were the limited-edition 911 Speedsters.

1990 TYPE 911 (L PROGRAM)

The new decade brought with it sweeping changes in the 911 product line. The C4 became the new flagship model, and the new Carrera 2 a rear-wheel-drive stablemate with nearly identical styling. The Speedster, Turbo, and Turbo Look models were discontinued for the 1990 model year. The C2 was offered with the new Porsche Tiptronic gearbox permitting either manual or automatic gear selection.

The assembly lines, having been converted to the new C4 coachwork, began to produce the new style Coupes, Targas, and Cabriolets for the 1991 model year.

1991 TYPE 911 (M PROGRAM)

The Turbo returned once more to the 911 fold, and the Carrera 4 was offered in Coupe, Targa, and Cabriolet versions. The C4 engine received new pistons, and the 3.3 Turbo engine was completely revised and developed 320 brake horsepower at 5,750 rpm and 450 lb-ft of torque at 4,500 rpm. The Turbo is equipped with its own dedicated suspension design, using MacPherson independent front suspension with light alloy transverse arms. The rear is independently suspended by track-correcting light-alloy semi-trailing arms. The cars were fitted for the first time with 17-inch wheels and 40-aspect-ratio rear tires.

As of February 1, 1991, all left-hand-drive 911 models are fitted with driver and passenger-side air bags as standard equipment.

1992 TYPE 911 (N PROGRAM)

Model proliferation began again as Porsche geared up to meet increasing demand for new 911 models. For 1992 there were four Type designations: 911 Carrera 2 Coupe, Targa, Cabriolet, and Turbo Look Cabriolet; 911 Carrera RS and 911 RS America Coupe; 911 Carrera 4 Coupe, Targa, and Cabriolet; and 911 Turbo Coupe.

The RS America was built specifically for the U.S. market, since the Carrera RS was not suitable to federal certification. The Carrera RS was designed for competition in Group N or Group GT. The America was a street version with C2 driveline technology, tuned suspension, 17-inch wheels, and a fixed spoiler (Turbo Look) as opposed to the new automatic Carrera wing. The RS is offered in three configurations (two of which can be licensed for the road), competition, touring, and one full race version.

1993 TYPE 911 (P PROGRAM)

The Turbo took a performance jump in midyear production with models produced after January 1993 powered by a new 3.6-liter engine developing 360 brake horsepower and 383 lb-ft of torque. Special Works also developed a Turbo S version with 381 brake horsepower. All Turbos featured new 18-inch wheels and revised suspension tuning. Beginning this year, all Porsche engines came with Shell TMO Synthetic engine oil SAE 5W-40. There were no significant changes to C2 or C4 models and this was the final year for the 964 version.

1994 TYPE 911 (R PROGRAM)

Reinventing the 911 in its own image once more, Zuffenhausen introduced the new Type 993 with revised front and rear styling, a high-output 3.6-liter boxer engine, six-speed manual transmission, a completely new rear suspension design, and a new, more luxurious interior. The 964 series Carrera 2 Cabriolet and Speedster were phased out as were the Targa and Turbo body options.

Output for the M64/05 engine was increased to 272 brake horsepower without changing displacement or compression ratio. The gains were achieved through lightened materials such as those used in the connecting rods, pressure cast aluminum cylinders with nickel-silicon bore surfaces, larger valves and passages in the cylinder heads, and a torsionally stiffer crankshaft. Lower exhaust back pressure also contributed to the increase in brake horsepower.

The suspension is also revised for the new Carrera models, and wider wheels are used all around with 20 millimeter wider tires on the rear. The new 911s are equipped with Porsche's ABS 5 antilock brake system, the most advanced ABS design in use.

For current models through 1998, refer to chapters eight and nine.

BIBLIOGRAPHY

Aichele, Tobias. *Porsche 911: Forever Young.* Indianapolis, IN: Beeman Jorganson, 1995.

Consumer Guide, ed. *Porsche Chronicle.* Chicago, IL: Publications International, 1995.

Leffingwell, Randy. *Porsche Legends.* Osceola, WI: Motorbooks International, 1995.

Ludvigsen, Karl. *Porsche: Excellence Was Expected.* Kutztown, PA: Auto Quarterly, 1977.

Rasmussen, Henry. *Porsches for the Road.* Osceola, WI: Motorbooks International, 1981.Seiffert, Reinhard. *Carrera 4.* Stuttgart, Germany: Porsche Cars AG, 1989.Starkey, John. *Porsche 911R, RS and RSR.* Osceola, WI: Motorbooks International, 1996.

INDEX